Praise for

Faith

"Eric Wilson is a trained and skilled Spiritual Director, a true contemplative, and a Christian deeply engaged in the travails of this world—a rare combination. Then throw in communication skills sharpened by theatre and pulpit—well, it is a unique and deeply needed voice."

 —**Randy Harris,** professor, Abilene Christian University, author of many books, including *Living Jesus, God Work,* and *Daring Faith*

"Energy, vitality, depth, warmth, and humor—Eric Wilson blends all these qualities in his life and his writing. *Faith: The First Seven Lessons* is a gift and a joy. You'll love reading it, and I'll be astonished if it doesn't make a tangible impact on your walk with God."

 —**Chris Webb,** Benedictine Anglican priest, former President of Renovaré USA, author of *Fire of the Word*

"In my fifteen years of working in and for the church, I'm not sure I've served alongside someone who has had the combination of spiritual maturity, wit, passion, and contagious love like Eric Wilson. He has chosen to live from the blessing of God, not for it; and because of this, he has an inviting presence that makes everyone feel like they are at home when they are with him."

 —**Josh Ross,** pastor, author of *Scarred Faith*

"Eric Wilson frames spiritual growth in the narrative of Christ, making it clear that our growth is not simply about individual fulfillment but is ultimately about participation in the Kingdom of God. Longing for direction in your desire for spiritual growth? Let Spiritual Director Eric Wilson be your guide."

 —**Sara Barton,** Chaplain, author of *A Woman Called*

D1059610

FAITH

FAITH

THE FIRST SEVEN LESSONS

ERIC LEROY WILSON

LEAFWOOD
PUBLISHERS
an imprint of Abilene Christian University Press

FAITH
The First Seven Lessons

LEAFWOOD
P U B L I S H E R S
an imprint of Abilene Christian University Press

Copyright © 2016 by Eric Leroy Wilson

ISBN 978-0-89112-348-4

Printed in the United States of America

Cover design by ThinkPen Design, LLC
Interior text design by Sandy Armstrong, Strong Design

Leafwood Publishers is an imprint of Abilene Christian University Press
ACU Box 29138
Abilene, Texas 79699

1-877-816-4455
www.leafwoodpublishers.com

16 17 18 19 20 21 22 / 7 6 5 4 3 2 1

Contents

PREFACE

Perhaps man has a hundred senses, and when he dies
the five senses that we know perish with him,
and the other ninety-five remain alive. . . .
Everything that is unattainable for us now will one day
be near and clear. . . . But we must work.

—*The Cherry Orchard*, Act II

THE FIRST DOMINO HAD ALREADY FALLEN. ANTON CHEKHOV tipped it long ago. He'd written plays in the late 1800s that seemed to capture a reality never before seen on stage. Before, there was pageantry, melodrama, and characters painted in broad strokes; but not so with Chekhov. Now on stage was the stuff of life that truly gets lived. His plays were not peopled with caricatures but were gatherings of seemingly real people dealing with real life issues. Each scene seethed with pressure building from the suffering, the anxiety, and the decisions, good or bad, that normal humans deal with daily. It was a new kind of theater.

It was a new kind of theater that demanded a new way of directing. In comes the great actor and director Constantin Stanislavski. As a director, Stanislavski figures out a way to get to the heart of a moment. He discovers how to find the beauty in the nuanced nature of each given moment on stage. It was a new way of directing.

It was a new way of directing that demanded a new kind of actor. In comes the great acting teacher Richard Boleslawski. Richard worked with actors to embody moments with the internal work of the characters' truest intention. The dominoes' path from writer to director to acting teacher is vast and has shaped so much of we see on stage and screen today.

But as impactful as this domino trail is in shaping world culture, it's nothing like the tipping point that took place in first-century Palestine when Jesus comes on the scene. Jesus comes not giving us a new way of looking at reality but gives us an entirely new reality in which to exist. "The time is fulfilled, and the kingdom of God is at hand" is the way Jesus would introduce this new reality—this Kingdom reality. No longer do we have to accept the reality of disconnection, injustice, and death. The doors of a new reality have swung open, and all who enter in will find wholeness, righteousness, and life. It was a new way of living.

And this new way of living demanded a new community in which to live. So all around the initial followers of Jesus' way, communities of faith began to pop up. Groups of gathered people sprang up everywhere. They began to eat together and pray together. These gathered people began to tell the stories and teachings of Jesus to one another. These communities of believers began to do things that instilled the ideas and truths of Jesus that ultimately lead to a new type of faith.

It was a new type of faith that demanded a new kind of actor. Because this wasn't the type of faith based on an acquisition of a series of beliefs. This was called The Way. It wasn't called The Beliefs.

This kingdom reality was a way of life. The faith Jesus espoused was a faith to be acted out. This was a vibrant, rich, active way of living and being.

Boleslawski spent quite a bit of time mentoring actors. These actors became well-suited for these new types of directors who were mounting these new types of plays. After many years of mentoring, Boleslawski set what he shared in these mentoring session in a book entitled, *Acting: The First Six Lessons*. It's an amazing book! It's one of those books you can read over and over again, discovering new nuggets with each new reading.

Faith: The First Seven Lessons is my attempt at collecting many of the ideas God unearthed for me as I mentored people over the last fifteen years. I have spent hours with grieving parents, broken-hearted lovers, angry church members, and young people trying to make sense of faith. Every hour spent was joy for me. What I have found to be true is that if two people come with a sincere attempt to seek God, often the Kingdom breaks out in their midst. The Holy Spirit moves and God's truth is revealed.

This book is a collection of ideas and concepts that come from the various Spiritual-Direction, executive-coaching, mentoring, and pastoral-counseling session I've had the honor of participating in.

I'd like to thank all who trusted me enough to walk with them on their journey of faith. Whether it was a block or several miles over many years, I'm grateful. I truly learned more from you than I've ever taught. And while I'm at it I'd like to thank all of the various performers, directors, set designers, and acting instructors I've had the privilege of learning about life from. In particular I'd like to thank Pastor Clyde Ruffin, who was mentor in both theater and faith in Christ.

To Randy Harris, Jerry Taylor, Josh Ross, Sara Barton, Chris Webb, Jane Willard, Mark Scandrette, and many others who have become partners in ministry in the past few years, I'm indebted to your gracious ears for helping me think out my faith as we work toward the kingdom reality together. And a special thanks to Teresa Klepac, who assisted me in turning my mad ramblings into a manuscript.

And none of my work in ministry would have occurred if it weren't for family support. To my parents, who have nurtured my thirst for reading and justice, I give thanks. Thanks to my brother Kevin for this three-or-four-year continued conversation about the unique way God has fashioned his universe for humanity's favor. Thanks also to Sharita, my wife. I truly have "found whom my soul loveth." I only know how to love others because of how you have allowed me to love you.

My prayer for us all is the same prayer Paul offered to the Ephesians: that

> the God of our Lord Jesus Christ, the glorious Father, may give you the Spirit of wisdom and revelation, so that you may know him better. I pray that the eyes of your heart may be enlightened in order that you may know the hope to which he has called you, the riches of his glorious inheritance in his holy people, and his incomparably great power for us who believe.

Or as the idealistic tutor Trofimov declares in *The Cherry Orchard*, "Everything that is unattainable for us now will one day be near and clear."

INTRODUCTION

Now on the next day Moses went into the tent of the testimony; and behold, the rod of Aaron for the house of Levi had sprouted and put forth buds and produced blossoms, and it bore ripe almonds. (Num. 17:8 NASU)

THE ENEMIES OF MOSES ARE RUNNING. THEIR PACE KEEPS TIME with the rhythm of their thinking: "What will we find? What will we find?" This has to be a morning like no other, maybe reminiscent of the day of Exodus. That same bated breath. The same muscle tautness as when bodies brace for who knows what. The Israelites, hell-bent on Moses's demise, approach the Tent of meeting.

Whether spoken or resting in the recesses of the human heart, right next to the unnecessary jealousy and the decaying resentment, festers the thought, *Who put you in control?* It is amazing. Get a group of people together, if only briefly, and the question of authority comes up. This is the issue that's bound to arise: *Who made you boss?*

What has God said? What will we find? Questions fly as the grumbling Israelites get nearer to the dwelling place of God. The answers to these questions will determine the course of the wandering Jewish nation. The answers will determine the trajectory of their journey. The long-awaited information that will finally put to rest the constant clashing between Moses and his followers lies just beyond the curtain of this tent where God's Presence is thick. They wait for any answer to arise.

The balance of power and control is such a tenuous thing in any community, because the ability to gauge correct levels of power and control is a tenuous thing in the human heart. I love to ask, "Is the dog wagging the tail, or is the tail wagging the dog?" because buried deep in so many of us is skepticism about who really is in control of our world, our nation, and our very hearts. All of us want to know: *Who made you boss?*

In the case of Moses, Aaron, and the children of Israel, the answer is simple: God. God conferred on Moses and Aaron the mantle of leadership when he spoke to Moses at that burning bush. Yet the Israelites questioned their leadership ever since the bush burned and the plan that spilled forth from the bush was set in motion.

The Israelites questioned the authority of Moses and Aaron, and so did Pharaoh. Quite sure that he held all the authority, the king of Egypt hurled at them the challenge, "Who are you to tell me to release these Hebrews who are held captive in my bondage?" After their release, the children of Israel at their first encounter with difficulty begin looking for a leader who will lead them back instead of pushing them forward. And that issue—the constant challenge of who calls the shots—becomes an echoing trope cutting gash marks in Moses's heart all through the tiresome journey to the

Promised Land. This is the issue in the air on this fateful morning when they all gather before the Tent of meeting.

To end their grumbling and complaining about who should wear the mantle of leadership he had given to Moses and Aaron, God intervenes with a challenge. "Get a walking staff from one leader of each of the twelve tribes, and get the famous one Aaron uses," God tells Moses. "Place all the rods before my Presence overnight." In the darkness of God's Presence, where mystery and power are often at play, the rods lie. These men wait to see what God will do to determine who is or is not in charge.

As is often the case when objects or individuals find their way before the Presence of God in night vigil, a change comes. One of the staffs, long ago cut from the trunk and root of its supporting tree, begins to grow. A branch that had experienced estrangement from its source of life for who knows how long, in the Presence of God receives new life. It turns out to be Aaron's rod. God confirms the role of Moses and Aaron as leaders by making Aaron's rod bud. Not only did it bud, but Numbers 17:8 says it "put forth buds and produced blossoms, and it bore ripe almonds" (NASB). Something seemingly dead displays full maturation, and produces an indication of life—a show of beauty—and fulfills its function of fruitfulness. While eleven rods lie dormant, one explodes with new life, beauty, and functionality.

This book is about how we grow. Not only how we grow, but about how all organic systems grow. This book attempts to address what we all need to bring to the table in order for real growth to occur, whether we face the task as a believer attempting to gain a greater sense of Christlikeness, as a person seeking greater spiritual acuity, or as an athlete, an entrepreneur, or an artist trying to reach new heights of achievement. For any organic system, whether a person or an institution, growth is necessary. But how many times have we reached for greater aims only to fail? Too often all of us have placed ourselves in environments and programs that promised development, only to fall far short. We have been to seminar after seminar and read book after book, only to look back at that experience as a good time and yet a time that promoted little, if any, growth.

The question this book attempts to answer is why. Why do some grow in those experiences and reach amazing heights of development, while others doing the same thing do not? How can we become the rods that blossom, bud, and bear good fruit? My contention is that without several key components, great opportunities for growth become great opportunities for wasted time, energy, and resources. With the infusion of seven powerful principles, however, growth becomes not only a possibility but an inevitability.

Growth, transformation, and transcendence have been a constant fascination for me. I discovered this almost by accident. By a magnificent turn of events, I became a playwright at the ripe age of twenty. In an attempt to earn enough credits to graduate from college, I assisted a professor and mentor with a project he was working on. My job was to gather research as he wrote a play. The play was a compilation of scenes and vignettes about the life of young, African American men. Whether it was because material was limited or my ability to do research was limited, I kept running into brick walls. So instead of coming to him empty-handed, I offered my instructor stories I began to write myself. From scraps of creased paper and phrases on the back of used napkins, I attempted to tell a story about the potential held in the human spirits of young men like me. The play was a success, and it propelled me into a career as a commissioned playwright.

Halfway through my career, I took an egotistical look at all the work I had produced. Instead of finding reasons to gloat and back-pat, I found a recurring statement I had never noticed in my works. Over and over in all of the work I had been doing for six or seven years, I had continually infused the same phrase: "This ain't the way things are supposed to be." It kept rolling out of the mouths of a variety of my characters—old sages, Pullman porters, a young girl trying to find her freedom by the Underground Railroad. All of them spoke from a place deep within themselves, "This ain't the way things are supposed to be." Without knowing it, I was trying to work out through my writing a tacit belief in the notion that there is more to be done, more to this world, more for us to become. Since then, whether as a playwright, educator, pastor, spiritual director, or executive coach, I have explored with others the concept of how people grow.

Growth, I believe, is a spiritual exercise. Real, profound, substantive change does not begin on a physical level. By necessity it is birthed from a spiritual reality. Growth comes from a place unseen but profoundly felt. Growth, transformation, and transcendence come from a place where one's character resides. If healthy and life-changing growth comes from a spiritual, unseen place, growth then is tied to a larger story of a good world being distorted, yet finding the path to return to goodness. Growth is framed in the larger narrative of the Christ, this historical figure who was as much God as he was man. The Christ, as defined in Scripture, is the very embodiment of the cosmic thought that holds all things together. My premise is that systemic growth is tied to who Christ is and what his larger plan for the cosmos entails, because, for growth to be sustained and long-lasting, it must be linked to something, or better yet, to someone larger than one's self. Why? Because totally self-focused change seldom has substantive sustainability. We will explore this interesting phenomenon in the chapters just ahead, but suffice it to say at this point that real growth is bound up in a really big story.

PART 1

PREPARING THE SOIL
FOR GROWTH
The Framing Story

Chapter One

WE WERE MADE FOR MORE

I WAS RAISED IN A FAMILY OF STRIVERS IN A TIME OF GREAT STRIVing. I was surrounded by people who took the initiative as well as the responsibility to make their lives and the lives of others better.

My father worked tirelessly to make a better life for our family. Our home became a haven for people who had found life to be an unforgiving friend. I really don't remember a time growing up when someone besides our immediate family was not living in our home. Uncles who lost their way and aunts who were broken by life brought with them a sack full of possessions and regrets. The faint smell of "let me start over again" emanated from every pore of every guest.

Our kitchen table became a confessional and then, after all the dishes were cleared, a spiritual surgical table. I was never privy to that discussion at that table because, as a child, I wasn't allowed to get into grown-folks' business. But once in a while, a scrap of wisdom fell from that table and, when it did, I savored those scraps as if they were a feast. I'll never forget one morsel of truth that fell from my mother's lips, passed an ailing aunt's ear, and landed on the floor for my grabbing. "If you know better, you ought to do better," my mother said. Those simple words were then and are now at the core of my life.

Within many of us burns a desire to do better and to be better. Within our "center place" simmers a desire to be transformed into something useful for a larger plan—a plan we hear in faint whispers inside ourselves. This "better" can be seen not only as a growing toward that better person but also as a return to that better being. We want to shake off behaviors and attitudes that are destructive to our selves, to others, and to the world we all occupy. Simultaneously, we desire to return to a nascent state of purity, connectedness, and trust. If these desires to improve are not heeded, they often atrophy, and those once powerful urgings for better are replaced by cankerous yearnings for self-gratification. But if even a faint wind of possibility kindles the embers of this desire, we warm to a notion deep within our very being that *we were made for more.*

Growth is a desire we have in ourselves and for ourselves. It's only natural that we have this desire for growth, because growth is a desire God has for us. There is not one father worth the title "father" who does not desire growth for his child. As a matter of fact, God throughout Scripture speaks words of encouragement into our consciousness in order to foster this desire to grow and become better. All through the Bible and all through our lives God places images before us to foster growth and transformation.

An Image to See

It is incredible how God continuously places before us an image of our higher selves. Before time began, God set in motion a series of events in order to place before you images of a better you, a braver you, a more centered and peaceful you. Jesus lays out the image of a better you before the world, all in the hope that we would embrace this thought that we can grow and be great. While sharing with his followers the greatness of his cousin and prophet John ben Zechariah (also known as John the Baptizer), Jesus places a greater image of humanity before us. He says,

> This is the one about whom it is written:
>> "I will send my messenger ahead of you,
>> who will prepare your way before you."
> I tell you the truth: Among those born of women there has not risen anyone greater than John the Baptist; yet he who is least in the kingdom of heaven is greater than he. From the days of John the Baptist until now, the kingdom of heaven has been forcefully advancing, and forceful men lay hold of it. For all the Prophets and the Law prophesied until John. And if you are willing to accept it, he is the Elijah who was to come. He who has ears, let him hear. (Matt. 11:10–15)

Jesus is saying that John is great. John is the representative incarnation of the greatest of all the former prophets, Elijah. That's high praise indeed. But what Jesus is also saying is that no matter how great John is, the smallest, seemingly most insignificant member of Christ's Kingdom is even greater in spiritual stature. When we are in the Kingdom, our potential for growth into greatness is unleashed. The small are no longer as small, and the seemingly insignificant now have enormous significance.

When Jesus says this about John the Baptist, is it possible that he is also revealing a secret that can change the world? Maybe he knows that when people begin to see this possibility for profound growth in the Kingdom, they will begin to aggressively storm in, saying, "I want in on this growth. I want in on this transformation.

I want in on this rich Kingdom life!" Why? Because in the Kingdom you can grow to greatness.

Jesus shows us an image of our greater selves and asks us to embrace it. We are not what our mistakes make us out to be. We are not who our bad decisions have led us to be. We are not what hatefully critical people attempt to label us to be. We are not even what our own negative self-talk fashions us to be. Once we aggressively find our place in the Christ-Kingdom, we are the inheritors of greatness. Once we are inside, God compels us to embrace the image of our higher selves.

The warrior-poet King David wrestles with this notion in a song penned centuries ago. As the melody springs to life and his voice dances over notes and rhythms, David marvels at this grander image of himself that God has placed before him:

> When I consider your heavens,
>> the work of your fingers,
> the moon and the stars,
>> which you have set in place,
> what is man that you are mindful of him,
>> the son of man that you care for him?
> You made him a little lower than the heavenly beings
>> and crowned him with glory and honor.
>
> You made him ruler over the works of your hands;
>> you put everything under his feet:
> all flocks and herds,
>> and the beasts of the field,
> the birds of the air,
>> and the fish of the sea,
>> all that swim the paths of the seas. (Ps. 8:3–8)

"God, you actually think of me," David ponders. In awed meditation David struggles to grasp this truth. "I am overwhelmed by the countless stars and the way planets stay in orbit," he sings. This orderly system functions and has functioned continuously in unfailing rhythms of rising and setting, rising and setting, all because you, God, have made it so. Isn't it incredible that Someone who can do all of this is concerned about someone as small as me, and not only is concerned about me but places me just a little lower than these heavenly bodies? Not only this, but David moves in his poem from heavenly bodies to heavenly beings, saying that God places us just a little lower in status than the angels themselves. No wonder David is forced to break out in song! David is wresting to embrace the God-given image of his higher self.

A Spirit to Dwell in Us

God places this image before us, and he also places his Spirit inside us. This is another means God employs to motivate our growth toward greatness. Within us is a sacred space where God's Spirit dwells, an interior shrine where the thoughts, feelings, consciousness, and desires of the Lord dwell. This is only natural, for the created always bears the consciousness of the one that created it. Even toasters, computers, and coffeemakers function with the thinking of the ones who created them. We are marked with the Creator's consciousness. We are imprinted with the fingerprints of the Divine. It is the sheer genius of God that suggests to us: Full access to my consciousness will reside in you once you completely commit to a lifestyle that can truly appreciate it. Imagine the uselessness of full access without full commitment. Upon commitment to Christ and the Christ-Kingdom project, Christians are gifted with the full Presence of God dwelling in them.

Just as a bank is only worth the amount that is in the vault, our value is determined by what is in us. What is in us is the very life-giving holy consciousness of God. We have within us an interior shrine where God resides, a sacred space and a quiet place where we and God can find rest together and commune in stillness, a place where he can impart his wisdom, grace, and peace. One of Christ's most active followers, Paul, describes it this way: "Do you not know that your body is a temple of the Holy Spirit who is in you, whom you have from God, and that you are not your own?" (1 Cor. 6:19). How does the "best you" function? Try to visualize this for a moment. How do you think? How do you behave? How do you speak? What one word describes how you function when you are being your best? Shout it out!

What I ask you to consider is a marvelously vital truth: This is not who you may or may not someday be. This is who you already are.

> Later, knowing that all was now completed, and so that the Scripture would be fulfilled, Jesus said, "I am thirsty." A jar of wine vinegar was there, so they soaked a sponge in it, put the sponge on a stalk of the hyssop plant, and lifted it to Jesus' lips. When he had received the drink, Jesus said, "It is finished." With that, he bowed his head and gave up his spirit. (John 19:28–30)

At that moment—the greatest eschatological moment this world has ever known—Jesus reconciled all things unto himself. Including you! With his death on the cross, Jesus the Christ put in motion the final piece that ushers in a profound reconnected-ness of all things—planets, stars, trees, birds, all thoughts, all beliefs, disparate policies, slugs, that melting snow mound on the top of Pike's Peak—all things, including you! Your job, and my job, is to see this as truth and begin acting accordingly. You are to live as if you have been ushered into the completed work of creation, to function from a platform where whatever God set in motion will soon come to pass. All you have to do is own your status as his beloved child and work in peace, knowing that his plan is quickly coming to a successful conclusion. Live as if you have been ushered into the completed work of the Lord, as a person who lives in God's eternal Sabbath rest.

Do you remember when the Sabbath concept first appears in the Bible? After every moment of major creative activity, Genesis says, "There was evening and there was morning." However, on the seventh day of Creation when God enters Sabbath rest, this sentence is noticeably absent.

> Thus the heavens and the earth were completed, and
> all their hosts. By the seventh day God completed His
> work which He had done, and He rested on the seventh
> day from all His work which He had done. Then God
> blessed the seventh day and sanctified it, because in it
> He rested from all His work which God had created and
> made. (Gen. 2:1–3)

God continues in his peace and shalom and invites us to see that while we work and live and love and do all of the things life requires, we can do them from a place of rest. We can do what we do from a place of peace, because God is bringing everything to fulfillment. Thus our work and life and love become an act of allowing God to do his thing instead of us forcing life to happen. Doesn't that sound like a better way of doing life? Hebrews 4:9 says, "So there remains a Sabbath rest for the people of God" (NASU). God wants us to grow because it is his desire that we all become active participants in undoing the Fall of humanity.

Chapter Two

UNDOING THE FALL

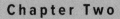

W E WERE MADE TO BE A "WE," BECAUSE, BEFORE THERE was time, God was a "We." God existed in community before time began. The essence of who God is gives us in effect a statement of community—and of healthy community at that. There the Creator was as a "We": God the Father, God the Son, God the Holy Spirit, functioning together, all existing on a common plain with a profound sense of unity. Yet in such a healthy way they functioned with enough room among themselves to be able to function together, although with independent function and personality. All you have to do is to look deeply into the first powerful verses of the epic of Genesis, letting the whirlwind of images and phrases and tones surround you.

In those verses you find yourself plunged into a torrent of ideas of God speaking worlds into being, darkness being torn asunder by the first dawning of light, and lush gardens being filled with every manner of flora and fauna. And in those creative moments we meet a God whose foundational essence is a "We." God is a "We," and he functioned as a "We"—fully united, fully focused, and fully in love. The love amongst that Trinitarian "We" was so rich and so sublime that their love could not be contained. Their love for one another burst forth, breaking through the boundaries of time and space and even heaven itself, as if some wave held back too long by levees and dams finally exploded with a force never before seen, never before equaled. God as the ever-loving "we" says, "Let *us* make man."

As God breathed life into humanity, God filled the human with the capacity for community. With that breath, God invited humanity into the pre-existent "we." God invited humanity into the circle of createdness, welcoming humanity into motion with stars, and moons, and flowing brooks, and waving blades of grass, and billowing clouds, and lions and ravens and speckled trout—all gazing at God, the ever-loving and eternal "We," waiting for him to count out the cadence so we can dance.

We were invited into the loving "we."

But let's see what happens after the Fall. Genesis 3:7–19 tells us,

> Then the eyes of both of them were opened, and they realized they were naked; so they sewed fig leaves together and made coverings for themselves.
>
> Then the man and his wife heard the sound of the Lord God as he was walking in the garden in the cool of the day, and they hid from the Lord God among the trees of the garden. But the Lord God called to the man, "Where are you?"
>
> He answered, "I heard you in the garden, and I was afraid because I was naked; so I hid."
>
> And He said, "Who told you that you were naked? Have you eaten from the tree that I commanded you not to eat from?"

The man said, "The woman you put here with me—
she gave me some fruit from the tree, and I ate it."

Then the LORD God said to the woman, "What is
this you have done?" The woman said, "The serpent
deceived me, and I ate."

So the LORD God said to the serpent, "Because you
have done this,

> Cursed are you above all the livestock
>> and all the wild animals!
> You will crawl on your belly
>> and you will eat dust
>> all the days of your life.
> And I will put enmity
>> between you and the woman,
>> and between your offspring and hers;
> he will crush your head,
>> and you will strike his heel."

To the woman he said,

> "I will greatly increase your pains in childbearing;
>> with pain you will give birth to children.
> Your desire will be for your husband,
>> and he will rule over you."

To Adam he said, "Because you listened to your wife
and ate from the tree about which I commanded you,
'You must not eat of it,'

> "Cursed is the ground because of you;
>> through painful toil you will eat of it
>> all the days of your life.
> It will produce thorns and thistles for you,

and you will eat the plants of the field.
By the sweat of your brow
     you will eat your food
until you return to the ground,
     since from it you were taken;
for dust you are
     and to dust you will return."

And there it happens, the cataclysmic moment of complete estrangement and disconnection! This is the moment when we ceased to be a "we." This is the moment when humanity's desire for the gratification of the "me" no longer allowed us to be a "we."

As a result, what do we see? Hiding from God. A covering from shame that previously never existed. God has to cry out, "Humanity, where are you?" I am absolutely convinced that a God who knows all things and sees all things was inquiring not about their present physical position but about their spiritual disposition. The question was not asked to clarify God's unknowing but humanity's undoing. God asks this profound question to get humanity to consider, "Look where you have put yourself." Are you in the dance? Are you centered in the circle of created-ness? Are you in the "we"? Or are you in hiding, mired down with a sense of shame? God said to them, "Where are you?" Immediately we see humanity disconnected from God.

What do we see Adam do at once? He blames his wife! Blame is one of the greatest indicators of estrangement. Blame says, "In order for me to distance myself from the consequences of our bad decision making, let me clarify the other's fault instead of my complicity." When this thought bubbles up from Adam's new-found brokenness, humanity experiences its first real disconnection from humanity, a disconnect from each other. Adam and Eve are no longer in step with one another. What is worse: they are no longer in step with their world.

Earlier their world graciously yielded all that was needed to sustain Adam and Eve—fruit, vegetables, shelter to shield, calm winds to cool. Now all of these necessities must be procured by great toil and labor, thus making cosmic estrangement complete. Humanity is now disconnected from creation itself.

The question is: who is dancing now? Asked another way: what happens when we cease to be a "we?" Think about the consequences of estrangement from God, when we cease to be a "we" and become a "me" and a "thee." What happens when humanity is no longer functioning naturally within the rhythms established by God, the Great Conductor? What happens when humanity is disconnected from its spiritual base?

Lost Wisdom

Several things happen, but one of the key consequences of a disconnection between humanity and God is a distancing from our source of wisdom and meaning.

I am a strong proponent of leveraging technology to help our aims, whatever those aims may be. So I have a lot of technology at my disposal. But I have an uncanny knack of not reading any of the directions on how to use all of the stuff I have. So I'm always fumbling around, trying to figure out how to use the computers and phones and iPads and such. I cannot tell you the number of documents I have lost or files I have corrupted because I did not take the time to really understand the operating systems. On those rare instances when I happen to actually look at the user manuals, I'm always thrown into this wonderment about how well things work once I grasp some understanding of how the operating system functions. I can't tell you how much joy came from the first time I used the Control, Alt, Delete buttons on my computer. "You mean I can actually undo a mistake?!" After that I started looking for the Control, Alt, Delete buttons on life itself. If only I could undo the cross words said, the decision made in haste, the zigs when I should have zagged.

Where is that understanding of the operating systems of life and the way it should be lived? It is found at the throne of God, because wisdom is birthed from the throne of God. In the very heart of God is the knowledge of how the cosmos itself operates. It's called wisdom. Steeped in the truth of God is a clarification of how life can function well. God is the only one that can provide true wisdom, for he is the only one with the correct amount of objective distance and longevity to clearly give a sense of how things can work well. The farther we are away from that source, the farther we are away from that understanding, the more likely we are to find ourselves stumbling about with fragmented, cluttered, and poorly wired lives. All the while God stands ready to usher us into a deeper sense of knowing. He calls all of us to a greater sense of centeredness and clarity. But are we willing to span the distance?

Lost Compassion

What happens when we cease to be a "we" and people are disconnected from people? What happens when we cease to be a "we" but become instead a "me" and them—when we are no longer connected with each other and creation? Here are just a few statistics:

There have been over fifty genocides in the twentieth century alone, atrocities in which one group of people viciously decimate another entire group of people. We are running through non-renewable resources faster than we could ever replace them. Twenty-two thousand children die each day due to poverty. Less than 1 percent of what the world spends every year on weapons would have put every child into school by the year 2000, and it didn't happen. Twenty percent of the world consumes over 76 percent of the world's resources. For every dollar in aid to developing countries, over twenty-five billion dollars is spent on debt repayment. Over ten years ago, globally seven hundred eighty billion dollars was spent to equip and finance the military, while at that time only six billion was spent on education, only nine billion was spent on water/sanitation, twelve billion on reproductive health of women, and thirteen billion on basic global health concerns. Just a paltry forty billion was apportioned for these global humanitarian concerns. In that same year those statistics were cited, Japan spent just about that same amount on entertainment alone.

Genocide, education, healthy environments, healing, and the promotion of life—are these issues God is interested in, that he cares about? Because the Israelites and specifically the leaders of the flock could not get their acts together, they were warned in Ezekiel 34:11–16 (NASU):

> Thus says the Lord GOD, "Behold, I Myself will search for My sheep and seek them out. As a shepherd cares for his herd in the day when he is among his scattered sheep, so I will care for My sheep and will deliver them from all the places to which they were scattered on a cloudy and gloomy day. I will bring them out from the peoples and gather them from the countries and bring them to their own land; and I will feed them on the mountains of Israel, by the streams, and in all the inhabited places of the land. I will feed them in a good pasture, and their grazing ground will be on the mountain heights of Israel. There they will lie down on good grazing ground and feed in rich pasture on the mountains of Israel. I will feed My flock and I will lead them to rest," declares the Lord GOD. "I will seek the lost, bring back

the scattered, bind up the broken and strengthen the
sick; but the fat and the strong I will destroy. I will feed
them with judgment."

Are these issues Christ is interested in? In Luke 4:18–19 (NASU), in
what must be the clearest and most concise mission statement of
Jesus's earthly ministry, he says:

"The Spirit of the Lord is upon Me
because He anointed Me to preach the gospel to the poor.
He has sent Me to proclaim release to the captives,
And recovery of sight to the blind,
To set free those who are oppressed,
To proclaim the favorable year of the Lord."

These are issues Christ is profoundly concerned with. Which is
amazing, isn't it? God cares about the small child sold into pros-
titution. His eyes are on the exposed ribs of the hungry and mal-
nourished. What's more amazing is how God intends to deal with
these issues of estrangement and disconnection.

Chapter Three

THE COVENANT PROMISE

GOD'S INTENTION IS TO END ALL OF THIS EVIL BY A COVE-nant—by a promise. The world's future hangs in the balance and its future rests on that promise. Just think about it. The possibility of ending all of our social and personal ills—the hope of undoing all the damage of the Fall—hinges on something as simple as one powerful promise from God.

This makes sense because a well-kept promise has the potential to transform lives. I am reminded of this when I recall the life of the courageous abolitionist Harriet Tubman. When our nation was mired in the "peculiar institution" of chattel slavery, there lived a woman with a promise. Oppressed by the horrid, mind-distorting, spirit-crushing, and body-destroying institution of slavery, one woman struck out for her own freedom. Harriet Tubman did not strive just to transcend and overcome her own enslavement, but she promised to return to help free others from slavery. She made that promise to her husband, who at the time when she escaped was unable to go. Through a torturous trek, Harriet managed to escape. Soon afterward she returned to help her husband and others as she promised, only to find that her own husband was not only unable to escape but was unwilling to escape. As we often say, a promise is a promise and, despite the crushing disappointment of her husband's inability to grow beyond his condition, Harriet kept her promise and ushered many to a place of newfound freedom, changing their lives immeasurably. A well-kept promise changes things.

This promise that God has made to end all of the conflict was given to a single solitary Middle Eastern man. Nothing was particularly astounding about the man. Nothing made him stand out more than any other Middle Eastern man in his generation, except one thing: this man named Abraham understood the power of faithfulness to a promise. If we took the time to extricate ourselves from the flimsy flightiness that is the hallmark of much of our world today, we too would see the richness and power of two people—based on who they are as individuals and who they are in relationship—making a binding agreement. Two people empowered and galvanized by the thought that this covenant we enter into this day we will uphold together, and nothing will stop us from fulfilling this pledge together. The power of a well-kept promise can change the world.

It's no wonder that God would use a covenant promise to make right a fallen world, because it was a lie in the garden that brought the whole Edenic consciousness crashing to a halt. God used the complete opposite of a lie to make right the wrongs perpetrated by the lie. We can once more be a fully reconciled and united "we" by the power of one covenant promise. That promise is this:

> The LORD had said to Abram, "Leave your country, your people and your father's household and go to the land I will show you.

"I will make you into a great nation
　　and I will bless you;
I will make your name great,
　　and you will be a blessing.
I will bless those who bless you,
　　and whoever curses you I will curse;
and all peoples on earth
　　will be blessed through you." (Gen. 12:1–3)

God will return us all to a state of "we-ness" and unity by creating a nation built upon this promise made to Abram. He will reconcile all things by the establishment of a Covenant Kingdom—a nation not so much predicated on a landmass but instead on a consciousness that spreads beyond borders and boundaries. God establishes a Covenant Kingdom based on a consciousness driven by this idea of relationship and blessings.

God's Righteousness

To truly understand the power of this Covenant Kingdom, you must come to understand a very specific attribute of God. One of his greatest characteristics or attributes is his righteousness or, in the original language of the sacred text Jesus read and quoted, God's *dikausuni theo*, which means his covenant faithfulness. Because God is righteous, he does only what is right and what is in keeping with his larger covenant plan. God promises to make everything right again, so every decision God makes is in keeping with the fulfillment of that promise. That is so amazing and so wonderfully comforting to know, because there are some decisions God makes about my life in particular that I just don't get. Or, more to the point, there are some decisions he makes about my life that I just don't like, and I am left with the heart-rending cry of *Why? Why would you do that to me?* Or *why would you allow this to happen to me?* What is so frustrating is that many times I do not get an answer. Or if I get one, it is given to me in such a way that is not clear or satisfying.

As I ponder God's *dikausuni*, as I consider his righteousness, I'm driven to the knowledge that while I may not be satisfied with God's decision making, or like it, or even understand it, I know the decision he made was in keeping with his larger promise and plan to return us all to a state of "we." While this return to a state of "we" may not make the dissatisfaction or confusion of the moment go away, it does take away a bit of the sting from the pain. And that lets me hang on long enough to see the necessity of his decision. Things unfold enough for me to say, "Oh, that must have been the reason that decision was made so many years ago." God makes decisions in keeping with his promise and plan. Failure is not an option because God doesn't fail.

God's righteousness demands fulfillment, and his righteousness dictates that he will do what he promised to do. This is expressed masterfully in a scripture that is quickly becoming one of my favorites. Listen to the power with which God expresses this thought through one of his prophets.

> Remember the former things, those of long ago;
>> I am God, and there is no other;
>> I am God, and there is none like me.
> I make known the end from the beginning,
>> from ancient times, what is still to come.
> I say: My purpose will stand,
>> and I will do all that I please.
> From the east I summon a bird of prey;
>> from a far-off land, a man to fulfill my purpose.
> What I have said, that will I bring about;
>> what I have planned, that will I do. (Isa. 46:9–11)

If God promises he will do it, he will do it! His own righteousness demands it. He will return us to this long-abandoned state of "we." It is a beautiful state to be in. It is amazing what his righteousness produces. His righteous commitment to the covenant promise that he made so many years ago produces an amazing state of connectedness.

God's Restoration

Look at the awesome picture that is painted of our return to "we-ness" as described in the last book of the Bible.

> After these things I looked, and behold, a great multitude which no one could count, from every nation and all tribes and peoples and tongues, standing before the throne and before the Lamb, clothed in white robes, and palm branches were in their hands; and they cry out with a loud voice, saying,
>
> "Salvation to our God who sits on the throne, and to the Lamb." And all the angels were standing around the throne and around the elders and the four living creatures; and they fell on their faces before the throne and worshiped God, saying,
>
> "Amen, blessing and glory and wisdom and thanksgiving and honor and power and might, be to our God forever and ever. Amen." And one of the elders answered, saying to me, "These who are clothed in the white robes, who are they, and where have they come from?" And said to him, "My lord, you know." And he said to me, "These are the ones who come out of the great tribulation, and they have washed their robes and made them white in the blood of the Lamb. For this reason, they are before the throne of God; and they

serve Him day and night in His temple; and He who sits on the throne will spread His tabernacle over them. They will hunger no longer, nor thirst anymore; nor will the sun beat down on them, nor any heat; for the Lamb in the center of the throne will be their shepherd, and will guide them to springs of the water of life; and God will wipe every tear from their eyes." (Rev. 7:9–17 NASB)

Then we find this in chapter 22 of Revelation:

Then he showed me a river of the water of life, clear as crystal, coming from the throne of God and of the Lamb, in the middle of its street. On either side of the river was the tree of life, bearing twelve kinds of fruit, yielding its fruit every month; and the leaves of the tree were for the healing of the nations. There will no longer be any curse; and the throne of God and of the Lamb will be in it, and His bond-servants will serve Him; they will see His face, and His name will be on their foreheads. And there will no longer be any night; and they will not have need of the light of a lamp nor the light of the sun, because the Lord God will illumine them; and they will reign forever and ever. (1–5 NASU)

Here we have a picture of all of the nations of the world, despite wars, deception, misunderstanding, and far too many curses cast, now together before the Christ. In their midst is a place of healing and life. It is a place where everyone wears the name of God because we are once again reconnected to our source.

This is the promise God has made to us. This is the promise or covenant that God invites us into. This is the bigger story our growth depends upon. However, the story is not the motivator. This story, while it is the richest ever told, is not what can drive our attempts at growth from start to finish. What can spark our attempts to grow and fuel the efforts until the end is the who, the how, and the when of our invitation into this promise.

The Promise Fulfilled

The Christ himself, the very source of reconciliation, invites us into this covenant promise. The Christ does it by the sacrifice he made on the cross, and he invites us into this awesome plan of return even while we are at our worst.

> God demonstrates His own love toward us, in that while we were yet sinners, Christ died for us. Much more then, having now been justified by His blood, we shall be saved from the wrath of God through Him. For if while we were enemies we were reconciled to God through the death of His Son, much more, having been reconciled, we shall be saved by His life. And not only this, but we also exult in God through our Lord Jesus Christ, through whom we have now received the reconciliation. (Rom. 5:8–11 NASU)

I have committed to working out again after years of failed attempts and false starts, but at this point I am giving it my all, and the exertion of energy expended is great. With this kind of work comes great sweat. I mean tons of it. I leave the gym drenched. I am sometimes greeted by my youngest son who could not care less that I stink and am wet with sweat and burdened with regrets of cakes eaten and calories consumed in the past. His arms are wide open for an embrace. *This* is a good image of the Christ. Open armed, he stands eager for embrace. He stands anxious to welcome us and invites us into his plan to transform all things in keeping with his larger covenant plan, even when we are at our filthiest.

So, the question that confronts us is this: What do we do in response to so great a faithfulness and love?

The answer is this: Enter into this promise, participate in it, and grow.

Chapter Four

BUT HOW DO WE GROW?

OR SPIRITUAL GROWTH TO OCCUR, IT IS ALWAYS IMPORTANT that we go to the source of all growth. It is important for us to see how Jesus grew people. Two things I see as key in Jesus's approach to soul-growing : 1) He believed that people grow as a part of a redemptive community. 2) He believed that he himself functions as a catalyst for growth and expanded capacity.

Let's first explore Jesus's invitation into redemptive community.

Jesus grew his followers in community. He graciously gave the people he encountered an invitation into a relationship of love, support, and growth. Jesus did not just send an edict from heaven, though he certainly could have. He did not send a messenger with a set of directives, though God had done so in the past. Instead, Jesus sent himself. He became human. He became manifest. He became the Tao incarnate. He became the *Logos* enfleshed. Why? Because what God desires is not merely the existence of knowledge but lived knowledge. This is the definition of wisdom. Jesus became the embodiment of wisdom—lived, enfleshed knowledge. When knowledge is enfleshed, we can get close to it and embrace it. Jesus wanted, and still wants, humanity to walk with wisdom down the street. He desires us to sleep alongside wisdom. He delights in those who sit and share a meal with wisdom as host and active participant at the table. This is what Jesus's first followers did. They walked with Jesus from town to town. They broke bread together and laughed together as they went along their way. This was a relational transfer of wisdom for his followers' growth, development, and expanded capacity.

Today we see this in play all over the world in communities that are experiencing healthy and sustained spiritual growth in their participants. People grow and capacity is expanded when individuals find themselves in redemptive community. A redemptive community is a group of people who find themselves joined together for the purpose of freeing themselves from all of the things that used to bind them. For some, the element that enslaved them had been substance abuse. For others, the binding element was unhealthy living. For some, the things that held them prisoner might have been dysfunctional relationships or distorted thinking, or all of the above. The participants are extricated from these life-restricting things when they naturally bump into redemptive components shared in their community.

I find that several redemptive components are integral to the spiritual growth and development of people. Five components that everyone needs to naturally encounter in a redemptive community are: Worship, Disciplines, Service, Mentorship, and the Normalization of Life Lived.

Worship

Worship becomes an integral part of growth because it gives participants an opportunity to rehearse for themselves who God is and who they are—all of this based on who God is.

When I use the word *rehearse,* I think about the definition a wise, old, acting teacher once gave. He said, "To rehearse is to re-hear and say." What a great definition for a theatrical rehearsal experience. In that time of practice, the actors are saying their lines, but they are also re-hearing the other players' lines. Over and over again, they re-hear and they re-say. So, when the performance is on, these lines become a part of who they are, and they naturally function as the characters they are to portray. Brilliant!

The same is true with our spiritual lives. When we participate in worship, we re-hear what God has done. We re-hear what God is telling us. In worship we also re-say. We repeat to ourselves and to those about us: God is all-knowing, he is all-powerful, he is ever-present, he is eternal, he is pure, he is righteous, he is holy, he is our rock, he is our shield, he is our fortress, he is our healer, he is the redeemer, he is the Maker and the sustainer of all that is. Over and over in worship, we re-hear and we re-say all of this, so that when the performance of life is on and struggles ensue, and troubles arise and success goes and then comes again, when a child goes wild and the sickness comes and life takes its necessary downs as well as ups, we naturally function as the character we are to portray. Worship is necessary in a redemptive community.

Spiritual Disciplines

Spiritual disciplines are an essential part of a redemptive community as well. I define spiritual disciplines as those biblically sound, time-tested, and effective practices that God uses to mold and shape our interior beings in the likeness of Christ. Such disciplines would include, but are not limited to

- Various forms of prayer
- Various forms of meditation, silence, solitude, or service
- Study of the Bible

- Specifically, the teachings of Jesus Christ
- Fasting of various kinds and lengths.

These disciplines function as means by which we place ourselves in the environment of growth where the Holy Spirit can continue the molding and shaping process that began so long ago to return humanity to its Edenic state. We enter into these disciplines and into this milieu with the knowledge "that He who began a good work in you will perfect it until the day of Christ Jesus" (Philip. 1:6 NASB).

Spiritual disciplines function on the principle of trajectory. What is "trajectory"? When Roger Staubach or Peyton Manning rifled a pass twenty yards downfield to a precise spot on a certain yard-line, they expected their receivers to know ahead of time what path the football would travel. That path was the ball's trajectory. If the receiver figured it out right, he would wind up in the right place to catch the pass. It was all a matter of trajectory.

Much of how you function with the Holy Spirit of God is through trajectory. You do not actually make or force things to happen when it comes to God and his larger redemptive plan, but you do have a role to play, and, I will add, a very important role to play. Our responsibility is not to force ourselves to grow. We know that one who attempts to will a plant to grow sets himself up for grave disappointment. A plant grows at the behest and in keeping with the rhythm set by God. Ours is not the responsibility to force our own growth, or to force our own purity, or to will our self with our own tenacity to stick to a moral code. No, our very important responsibility is to place our selves in the trajectory of God's will so that he can gift us with growth, purity, and a status of being where we naturally become the kind of people who adhere to a moral code. While we are trying to grow in Christ, we must always remember that "every good thing given and every perfect gift is from above, coming down from the Father of lights, with whom there is no variation or shifting shadow" (Jas. 1:17 NASB).

Growth, purity, strength, wisdom, a higher-self, mindfulness, and keen awareness come from God. But it is our responsibility to place ourselves in situations that facilitate God's ability to give us these gifts. Baptism is placing one's self in a trajectory to receive the gift of justification, sanctification, eternal life, and the gift of God's Spirit. Communion is placing ourselves in a trajectory to be ushered in to table fellowship with God and other believers—the kind of fellowship that hinges on the Christ who sacrifices all to get us to that table. Prayer is placing ourselves in a trajectory to be heard and to offer an open awareness to God for him to speak to us. All of these spiritual disciplines that we employ are but ways to place ourselves in God's trajectory for him to give us the gifts the Father of light longs for us to have.

Service

Something incredible occurs when we care for others. It is when we serve that we find ourselves on the altar of transformation. While we target others intending to help them as the recipients of our service and care, it is the servant who is redeemed. When we place ourselves in an environment to serve others who require much more than we ourselves have to give, when we face insurmountable needs with shallow pockets, when we bear the weight of suffering far too great to endure, it is in such moments that we are freed from the slavery of doubt and move toward the freedom of greater trust in God. In those sacred moments, God's abundant nature breaks through and providence lays waste our wants.

I find this to be true every time I run toward a daunting fight. Whether it is reaching out to a hurting community of people in active recovery from addictions, or teaching those fresh out of incarceration, or counseling sessions with the emotionally or spiritually broken, I go in with the full knowledge of my incompetence. They have had encounters in their past that bring pressure to bear on what we're trying to accomplish, but those events may never come to light. They have had experiences that go unspoken but are actively in play as we engage. Pockets of my own brokenness that I am well aware of but have gone unaddressed may bubble up unexpectedly during that moment. Knowing that things like this will be in play, still you stand in the gap. You avail yourself of the moment. Knowing, as Walter Mosley so aptly put it in the title of one of his novels, that you are always outgunned and outmatched, still you give yourself over to the unrelenting moment. Much like the boy with the few loaves and fish in Scripture, I bring the little I have in service of the multitude of anxieties and concerns of the individual, community, or world in the hope that in the hands of Jesus my failings can be made into a feast for many. It occurs. I go in with the full knowledge of my incompetence but also with the full knowledge that God is sufficient.

God performs. Jesus multiplies. He keeps pulling out of the bits and pieces of our scatteredness enough to feed somehow. The right word is said. The right scripture is brought to bear. That occurrence in your life you have always wondered why it happened becomes the very point of association that brings healing to the hurting. The phone call comes in out of the blue with words or resources you desperately need to bring care to those in need. All of a sudden your capacity for trust grows. Your trust in God deepens. And the ropes that hold you in the place of doubt are loosened—sometimes completely, sometimes just a bit. At that point, we are released from the faithful nature of our unfaithfulness.

Mentorship

Doing "faith" with one another is active resistance against the notion that we are made for isolation. Once again, we must always remember, the Fall was about estrangement and the insidious nature of isolation. As long as we buy into the lie that we are not a "we," sin will always have full reign. Oppression seems so much easier to commit when a clear distinction is made between the other and ourselves. One of the greatest strategies employed for the enslavement and exploitation of the African American was the media's insistence that these indigenous people of African descent were beasts.

While we were in Washington, DC, my wife and I went on a hunt for records of her family lineage. After hours of research and combing through archives, we found the records of the slave master who owned my wife's distant relatives. As we got closer and closer to our goal, the beating of our hearts got heavier. Our bated breath became shallower as we homed in on the coveted entry. We moved from state to region, then from region to town, and finally from town to plantations. One after the other, we dug deeper into years and dates. We then stumbled upon the document that inventoried the slave master's belongings: Two homes, twenty head of cattle, three mules, and the list of owned humanity. This list of names of human beings was numbered only after the draft horses and livestock. How could this happen? How could God's crowning achievement of creation be relegated to mere livestock?

To understand the list, you must come to understand the media campaign that accompanied the enslavement of human beings. Throughout literature, lectures, pulpits, art work, and minstrel shows, an onslaught of messages claimed the inferiority and bestial nature of the enslaved. If you hear that message long enough and loud enough from a barrage of sources, the lie becomes the truth. The message hangs thick in the air. The lie sticks to our clothes and becomes embedded in our ethos. The message divided us somehow. The "we" of humanity became an us and a them. The "them" could then easily be placed on a list that held household goods along with humanity. What an anathema to God's divine plan of oneness, wholeness, and unity.

But not so with mentorship.

Mentorship is the rebellious claim that we cannot and will not make it without one another. Our growth and development into Christlikeness is incumbent upon the linking of lives as well as the embrace of the other. I have had the distinct honor of mentoring across cultural, gender, as well as generational lines. There is nothing greater that heals the brokenness of our collective, uniquely American sin-stain of slavery than spiritual growth together. There is no need for forgetfulness and denial of our past, whether it is individual or collective transgression. There is an ardent need for each of us to partner with God and each other to facilitate the growth and development of our interior selves. This is the miraculous nature of mentorship.

The "me" others see is a far cry from who I was in the past. The trail of transgressions that lies in the wake of my youth is too numerous to name at this point. The list is only exacerbated by the fact that I knew better. There was a *Logos*, a Tao, a gifted, high moral compass residing deep within me that made me know full well that what I was doing was wrong. So, forgiveness was a hard concept for me to wrap my mind around. I understood penitence. I had a great grasp of shame. But forgiveness eluded me. Mind you, I grasped God's forgiveness through the blood of Christ Jesus intellectually, but intellectual ascent in regards to forgiveness seldom leads to peace or productive service to the Kingdom.

Something amazing happened one time while I was mentoring a young person struggling with the sin in her life. After watching this young lady beat herself up like a professional prizefighter shadow boxing—with the shadow winning, I grabbed her hand. I looked her deeply in the eye and spoke into her life these words: "Your sins are forgiven!"

This is one of the greatest gifts we can give to those we mentor. Listening to confession and speaking words of forgiveness is a boon, it is a balm—it is verbal embrace from Jesus through the mentor. That girl's life changed from that point on. But my main point here is that my life changed as well. Those words I spoke to her moved my understanding of forgiveness from my head to my heart.

Life Lived

I don't think it was happenstance that Jesus was born in meager surroundings. I don't think the manger was an afterthought of God. I think Christ's being born in ordinary surroundings is an intrinsic part of the divine narrative and a critical part to the story, because ultimately the divine is experienced from living the ordinariness of our workaday lives. If we seek God only in those rarified moments of ecstatic experience, we miss out on much of God's omnipresence. God is everywhere and all of him is everywhere at all times. So while we may catch a clearer glimpse of his majestic nature as we look out at the vastness of the crashing waves of the expansive sea, or witness this steadfastness when we throw our heads back in awe as we strain to gaze at mountain peaks, God ultimately is found in the ordinary. He is experienced in the mundane. The fullness of God and his transformative hand are employed in the everyday-ness of life lived.

I am indebted to Kathleen Norris who wrote *The Quotidian Mysteries: Laundry, Liturgy and "Women's Work."* In this small, yet powerful and poetic work, Norris drops amazing little bread crumbs that lead to an understanding of the sacredness of the ordinary. She led me to understand that if we wait for the burning bushes of life in order to hear God, we are wasting so much of our time here on Earth. This is certainly a God-bathed world, as Dallas Willard reminds us. God speaks, and God speaks everywhere, and at all times.

As I worked through Norris's book, I began to clean our little condo differently. Truth be told, for me to consistently participate in cleaning was different in itself—a fact that my wife would vigorously attest to. I started getting up early in the morning and thoroughly cleaning our kitchen. But I would do it as a sacred act. Previously, if I mopped, I neglected the spaces that were hard to get to or that are seldom seen by the casual eye. Now this became my passion—to pull out the refrigerator enough to expose the dirt that collects in the hidden places and shed light on the dirt that cakes and concretes even more because it's always unnoticed. Cleaning there and cleaning that was now for me a sacred act because I realized how much interior dirt can build up in me in the darkness. If I neglected the dirt behind the refrigerator or the stains that collected behind the stove, it would make it that much easier to turn a blind eye to the sins of jealousy, resentment, and hate that collect in the corners of my consciousness.

So I began cleaning in celebration of God's gracious willingness to move some things in my life in order to get to what needed to be cleaned in me. I folded clothes with a greater degree of care and concern. Not because anyone noticed or offered kudos for a job well-done: I folded clothes better in praise of a God who brought order to my all-too-often unruly life. Cleaning became my act of worship and praise to God. Daily chores developed into a means by which I could understand God as well as understand myself. All of a sudden, the housework I loathed to do became a means for me to get closer to God and gain a better understanding of him. Please, don't celebrate my cleaning prowess too much. That experiment with housecleaning lasted about as long as it took me to read Kathleen Norris's book and, as I say, thank goodness it was a very short book! That book, as well as my foray into cleaning, helped me to realize that you encounter God in life lived.

Let me hurry to say here that, to encounter God in life lived, you need two important things. First, you need a mindfulness and awareness that looks for God in the ordinary. The shepherds during Christ's birth had this kind of mindfulness. These men possessed a sense of awareness made sharp by their profession. They were well-versed in taking note of things in their surroundings. The safety of their flock required an awareness to change, adjustments, and oddities in the environment. Where is the freshest grass for grazing? Is there a burr lodged deep in some sheep's wool? Is the flock fearful or walking with a sense of calm? Such critical questions that determine the condition of the flock are only answered with an acute sense of awareness. No wonder they were some of the first to hold vigil over the Christ's birth even in the midst of the ordinariness of the manger and livestock.

The call here is for us to live expectantly. Where and when will the divine break into the mundane? We should be constantly on the lookout for the sacred to invade the secular. We are to live knowing that around any corner or in the midst of any encounter God may be speaking or revealing. We work, play, and live, constantly asking, *Where can I see your hand, dear Lord? From what source will I hear your voice?*

The second thing required is for us to walk with someone who is willing to be our spiritual docent. There are so many jobs I would love to do. So many roles I would love to fill, if only for a brief moment. One such job is that of a museum docent. The docent serves as a guide through the museum. Fully aware of the ins and outs of each exhibit, the docent provides an appreciation for every work of art they engage. Docents assist the museum visitors with greater insight into each work they view. What an exhilarating role to play, to serve as a cheerleader for Matisse! What a gratifying responsibility, to expose others to the subtle sublimity of the Impressionists! What a job, to walk visitors through the blues that emanate from a collage of Bearden. But each of those activities pale in comparison to serving as a spiritual docent, to walk through the gallery of someone's life and give her an appreciation for the works that make up her life. Whether the person sees his life as mundane or if each picture seems to be an image of chaos, the spiritual docent walks people through the exhibits that make up their lives and celebrates with them each vibrant or muted hue.

When we have someone we trust to bring a healthy, God-honoring perspective to the events of our lives, we begin to see the divine hand everywhere. Whether that person is a minister, mentor, spiritual director, Christian coach, or a soul-friend, their role is to assist you in seeing God's hand in your everyday life—because life happens, doesn't it? She says, "I do." Your employer says, "You're fired." The kids win soccer tournaments, and they get cut from the team. Illness comes and divine intervention either is seen or is conspicuously absent. Life happens.

How do we make sense of those happenings? Answering that question in the presence of someone with a listening ear inclined toward you and the Spirit of God can foster unparalleled growth in his redemptive community. As we are ushered in and find our way into that redemptive community, there is a crucial truth we must keep in the forefront of our minds. This unshakable truth is that ultimately Jesus is the catalyst for our growth.

Chapter Five

JESUS AS CATALYST FOR GROWTH

THE LANGUAGE OF MARK IS REMARKABLY INTERESTING AS IT relates to relationship and expanded capacity. Listen to how Mark explains the appointment of the twelve men who become apostles. He tells us that Jesus "went up on the mountain and summoned those whom He Himself wanted, and they came to Him. And He appointed twelve, so that they would be with Him and that He could send them out to preach, and to have authority to cast out the demons" (3:13–15 NASB). They had to learn how to carry out two important functions. The Twelve had a proclaiming function, and they had a healing function.

These failed and faulty men were given the responsibility to carry the message of the Kingdom of God. These men—several fishermen, a political dissident, and a former conspirator with the Roman enemy—were given the charge to spread the message of Christ. They were entrusted with the message of life that would ultimately bring salvation to the entire cosmos. Not only this, but these men were commissioned to bring healing to the human body. Diseases that at that time had no cure, diseases that not only destroyed body but marginalized the afflicted from society, diseases that had spiritual implication to the one stricken, were supposed to be eradicated by the healing touch of these ordinary and fundamentally flawed men.

How would they be able to do it? What would enable them to move out into a hungry and needy community with such faith to believe it would even be possible? What is the means by which these men could be empowered and informed to such a degree that they could believe they could fulfill such an incredible charge?

The answer to this question comes from how Jesus grew people. You see, Jesus functioned on the assumption that people grow in a redemptive community. He intrinsically believed that if they could just be with him, they would learn what they needed to learn in order to fulfill their expected aims. Before a word was to be proclaimed and before one person would be healed by his followers, they needed to be with him. Jesus believed that people grow in formative community.

When anyone accepted the invitation to ascend to the mountain to be with Jesus, they encountered a specific kind of learning environment, because Christ would teach them in a very specific way. How did Jesus teach his followers? This is the question we must consider here. As the incredible works of Kieth Anderson have shown me, Jesus taught those in the formative and redemptive community in several ways.

Jesus Taught Them Rabbinically

Jesus was a rabbi. Rabbis teach by encouraging their students to think scripturally. The rabbi asks the students questions and engages them in ongoing dialogues, forcing them to wrestle with ideas and concepts and challenging them to consider how these concepts and ideas apply to life lived.

When I think of a rabbinical teaching style, my mind immediately goes to the peripatetic schools of Plato and Aristotle. These schools were characterized by a philosopher gathering a group of students and simply walking with them. They walked together in community. They wandered through gardens and city streets and pondered ideas as they walked. As they walked, they took in their surroundings and allowed the context they walked in to shape what they learned. Life itself was the great backdrop of their learning. Life also was the visual aid by which they contemplated crucial issues and gained greater understanding of what was being taught. The philosopher asked questions and allowed his students to talk out the thought the teacher was attempting to pass on.

Jesus, in a truly incarnational way, likewise walked with his men and carried them through life lived to pass on to them the critical information they needed to bring salvation and healing to the world.

Jesus Taught Sacramentally

Jesus as God makes things sacred. He chooses the common things in life and sets them aside for divine use. This is at its core what sanctification means—that God chooses the typical and ordinary things of life and sets them aside and makes them sacred for divine purpose.

For example, Jesus takes his students to a wedding. Fully present and engaged in the ordinary stuff of life like a marriage ceremony, there they discover a need. There is not enough wine. In this moment of life being lived, we have a social dilemma. No one runs out of wine at a wedding feast. As a matter of fact, the typical family would have to buy so much wine that they would buy the cheapest available. This would be like going to a huge retail store that sells in bulk and buying boxes and boxes of inexpensive stock because the last thing they want to do is to run out. They know their wine is cheap so, to mask its lack of quality, they put out a little of the better vintage wine first. Then the guests, after drinking it, will be so inebriated that they won't even notice the substandard quality of the bulk wine. If a couple and their families ran out of wine on such an occasion, they would be known in the synagogue as "those people that ran out of wine at the wedding." Conversations about them from then on would be shaped by their shortsightedness and failure. Word around the Temple would be, "I don't know if we can trust that family. You remember they were the ones who didn't have enough wine at their child's wedding." So much is at stake for this family in this moment. The moment they find out the wine is running out, thoughts of a ruined future come crashing down on them. Right at a time when their hearts should be glad. Their hearts career from the heights of great joy to the depths of possibly becoming social outcasts once the last drop of wine is poured.

Jesus sanctifies this moment. He sets it aside for divine usage. He repurposes the vessels used for the ceremonial cleaning of hands and uses them as sacred vessels of the miraculous. Jesus changes water into wine before that amazed and relieved family, and he uses this as a teachable moment for his students, who soon will be unleashed into a world that desperately needs transformation to occur in their empty vessels of life. Jesus uses this sacramental means to teach them and to form them. Later Jesus uses fish and loaves. He uses the washing of feet. He makes sacred the ordinary in order for his students to be shaped by these sacramental means.

We too are formed in such ways. Simple table fellowship of broken bread and blessed wine is made sacred to form us in community with Christ. Participating in and witnessing the simple act of being immersed in water made sacred by God forms us and shapes us in our faith communities. All of these, plus many others, become the sacramental means by which we are educated in community with Christ.

Jesus Grew Them Missionally

Jesus sent his students out to fulfill his mission to expand the Kingdom of God. Jesus was well aware of the power of mission. With an embrace of mission, there is purpose. With an embrace of mission, there is a sense of ownership. With an embrace of mission, we find ourselves embedded in something as transient as the fleeting moment but as eternal as the ever-unfolding story of the universe itself. So Jesus insisted on sending his followers out to engage the world with the larger mission of the Kingdom of God. What started off with a promise made to Abraham thousands of years before now served as the very function of Jesus's learning community. They were to go out and be the blessing that spread from Abraham's seed. So Jesus sent them out.

I love his radical stance as it relates to sending out his students. Don't take anything with you, he told them. Rely on the provisions God provides and the people you encounter. Dive out there with little so that I can expand your capacity for faith, because with greater trust comes greater confidence in the message you are sharing. This message I send you out to spread is not one of theory or conceptual concern. The message I have sent you to spread is the message you are to live and rely on.

So these men went. Scripture says they went in pairs. They taught, healed, and released people from the evil impulses that once controlled them. With great joy they returned from going out, knowing that what they were learning had real present-day application. I learned the significance of this in graduate school. In an environment that thrived on concepts that may or may not have any significance in real-world application, I thrived. I went to school for theater. I stumbled upon a place right beside some of the greatest minds in the philosophy of performance. I sat across from preeminent scholars in fields I had never heard anything about. These professors were flying around the world to talk about amazing and heady topics concerning postmodernism, militant feminist theory, translators of obscure texts from even more obscure playwrights. Those professors gathered around themselves students pursuing even more interesting and bizarre topics of study. Then, here comes the kid from the wrong side of the tracks, a guy who happened to write a wildly popular play, purely by accident! I thought a graduate program in theater would give me an opportunity to write more plays and perform in more shows, only to discover that the program I found myself in was heavily into theory and philosophy. The thing is, I loved it. I had spent four or five years actually doing the craft versus spending that amount of time merely talking about it, so the questions I would ask and the discussions I would prompt were solely about what can work in real-life circumstances.

What I discovered was that all of these professors who devoted their lives to performance were enthralled by returning to their first love—not just talking about a subject but being fully engaged in doing the very thing they loved. Intrinsically, they knew that theory and concept are only as good as what you can resonate in real-life circumstances. What mattered was what could work on stage.

As we perform the Kingdom work of God, we must not focus solely on theories, concepts, and sacred discussion, because real learning occurs when we are actively engaged in participation in the Jesus project. Jesus, of course, knew this, and we see him sending his learning community out to heal and teach. They came back to unpack what occurred as they participated in the mission, and then Jesus sent them out again. We see this wonderful combination of sending out and coming back. The sending out was to experience the Holy Spirit in action and the coming back in was a means of placing what they encountered in the larger context of their individual and collective presence in the larger story of God's redemption.

Jesus Grew Them Teleologically

Jesus had in the forefront of his mind what his students ultimately were to become. He was focused on their *telos*. *Telos* is an amazing Greek word. It is a word that has brought healing and perspective to me in my walk with Christ. *Telos* is the end result. *Telos* represents what God has already determined us to be. In the mind of God he has images of who you and I are ultimately meant to be. He holds our fully realized "being-ness" in the place of his mind where he keeps all things holy. There is a holy "you." There is a fully realized "you." There is a "you" that God is actively pursuing, molding, and shaping you into. I find so much comfort in the words of the apostle Paul when he says that he is "confident of this, that he who began a good work in you will carry it on to completion until the day of Christ Jesus" (Philip. 1:6). God has not stopped, nor will he ever stop, working on you, molding you, and shaping you into what he intends. What amazing changes will take place! Paul later on tells us that we will be changed, and it will happen "in a moment, in the twinkling of an eye, at the last trumpet; for the trumpet will sound, and the dead will be raised imperishable, and we will be changed" (1 Cor. 15:52 NASB).

God has in his mind the ultimate you he has destined you to be. Jesus worked actively to foster experiences that shaped his followers in this teleological image, and he continues to do so today with us. Some rough edges must be made smooth. Some holes need to be filled. Some attitudes and mindsets must be adjusted or outright jettisoned. Jesus is that catalyst of change.

Without question there is much for us to do. We are to pursue holiness. We are to actively work toward our sanctification. If sin is to be lessened and character developed, this will not occur through passivity or luck. No, we must play a role in our growth and development. As we do these things, we must never forget that God, in the person of Jesus Christ and in the power of the Holy Spirit, is doing the lion's share of the work. Once again, our job is placing ourselves in the trajectory of our growth in faith. It is God's task to grow us. To attempt it any other way leads us further from God. When we attempt to grow ourselves, we tend to become arrogant, self-righteous, and unfit for the unity God ultimately desires for us all. Transcendence is birthed from a divine source.

Chapter Six

WHAT IF WE DO NOT GROW?

WHAT ARE THE CONSEQUENCES WHEN WE DO NOT ANSWER the invitation into Christ's redemptive community?

Late in the winter of 2010 an interesting incident occurred on a peninsula in Lake Erie, an incident that creates a compelling image of faith in some of us. There it is, braving the frigid frost and high tide of Lake Erie. A lighthouse. Much like all lighthouses, its charge is to keep ships tossed about by the winter waves safe from the rocks.

Lighthouses function on a practical and psychological level. The light cast from a lighthouse shows sailors specifically where lie the treacherous obstacles that might impede their journey. But, more than this, the lighthouse serves as an indicator that a safe route does, in fact, exist. A safe harbor is in the offing. While the waves may crash and the waters may surge, the lighthouse assures the sailors that someone is looking out for their best interests. This message is what the stalwart nature of a lighthouse proclaims.

But something went very wrong during the winter of 2010. With the weather so cold, the wind so high, and the waves so strong, ice began to cover the base of that Lake Erie lighthouse. As ice tends to do, ice began to collect on the ice. Then the ice began to climb, first on the base and then on the front of the light-house. On the front and then toward the back, the ice formed in a frigid covering. Soon the ice encased the entire lighthouse, and, in the deadly Michigan cold, no ship or boat could rely on its hope-producing light.

This is sad but apt picture of some of our churches today. If we take a passing glance at some of the major world crises we cataloged earlier—disasters such as genocide, poverty, the vast proliferation of arms, generations of peoples around the world stripped of their dignity, forced to resort to terrorism and to rage against oppression—we find our churches focusing their energies elsewhere. Those churches act as if they are frozen and without a notion to cast their light in those dark storms.

If we just glance at what many of our churches have focused on while these world crises rage, we will find a list that includes worship styles, who can participate in church life, music styles, who is scripturally right and who is scripturally wrong, or which political view is right and which one is wrong. None of these topics are bad topics to discuss. In light of the storm that is raging in the world, though, those may be topics to discuss after the storms subside.

What happens when the people of God are frozen over and are unable to shine their light of solution and life? What happens when the Kingdom people of God are not engaged with the Kingdom work of God? The prophets of old spoke of such times in blazing tomes and fiery refrains.

Will not the day of the LORD be darkness instead of light,
Even gloom with no brightness in it?

"I hate, I reject your festivals,
 Nor do I delight in your solemn assemblies.
"Even though you offer up to Me burnt offerings and
 your grain offerings,
 I will not accept them;
And I will not even look at the peace offerings of your
  fatlings.
"Take away from Me the noise of your songs;
 I will not even listen to the sound of your harps.
"But let justice roll down like waters
 And righteousness like an ever-flowing stream.
       (Amos 5:20–24 NASU)

Trust me, at this time these Kingdom people got their worship forms right. They got ceremonial adherence right. They were mindful to ensure that they carried out all of the specifics of their worship and sacrifice correct to the letter. God was not dissatisfied with how they worshiped him. God's concern was not that they were worshiping wrong. His concern was that the function of worship, the development of the natural outpouring of justice and righteousness, was not taking place.

We see the same thing happening in the New Testament. The Kingdom people of God were going above and beyond the call of duty as it related to religious adherence to rule-keeping. The Pharisees and scribes specialized in following the rules and regulations put forth. But Jesus warned them, "Woe to you, scribes and Pharisees, hypocrites! For you tithe mint and dill and cummin, and have neglected the weightier provisions of the law: justice and mercy and faithfulness; but these are the things you should have done without neglecting the others" (Matt. 23:23 NASU). Worship and all forms of spiritual discipline and religious adherence are but sacramental means by which our hearts are shaped to be conduits for justice, mercy, and faithfulness. They are not the thing. They are the thing that gets us to the most important thing. As we look at the world-crisis statistics we cited earlier, we must ask ourselves if we are discussing these topics as we gather in our faith communities. Are we examining how the word of God can be spoken to address some of these major concerns? As we look at the statistics again, we must ask ourselves as Kingdom people if we are fully engaged in Kingdom business.

But let us not use this as a means to sink into guilt, shame, and dismay. Let us not use this as a moment to cast stones at the bride of Christ. For regardless of the condition of the bride, Christ has chosen her to be his own. Instead, we look at this common occurrence of being in the Kingdom but not of the Kingdom to lead us to an important question. That question is, why? Why do we find ourselves so often as God's people on the sidelines of doing God's business? This is a question we must ask over and over again, because this will be a perennial problem until Christ returns. Why do we often find ourselves in the Kingdom but not of the Kingdom?

With Scripture, many scholars, and life-lived to back me up, it is my contention that while it is in our very make-up to do Kingdom work, often our hearts become corrupted as we make our way in this fallen world. The human heart or spirit is seen as the seat or center of our cognitive, emotional, decision making, and will-seeking activity. The longer our hearts exist in dysfunctional situations, experience trauma and neglect, or merely inherit the consequences of others' bad decision-making, the more our hearts become distorted.

Janice came to me to discuss her abusive marriage. She spoke of the horrors of waking up to a man standing over her, yelling obscenities because of her inability to live up to unexpressed expectations that, if expressed, would have certainly been unrealistic. She had lived with this burden for years. Her heart that once craved to teach children and take in the hurting had been distorted into a heart that merely wanted to survive.

As I listened to her numerous stories of violence and hiding in dark corners of closets only to be found, a thought weighed heavy in my spirit. A burden crushed me as I took in every story. It wasn't the sadness that I felt for her, although that was certainly there. It wasn't the sense of being overwhelmed by the task at hand, although that was certainly a reality that needed to be faced at a later time. I soon realized that the weight I felt was a sense of discernment about the condition of Janice's heart. With further questioning, I discovered that her distorted heart believed this abuse was all she deserved. Being in that toxic environment where she had existed for so long, her heart began to agree with the blows from his fist. Her heart nodded in acceptance of the curses and false claims. Janice's thoughts, emotions, conscience, and will acquiesced to the hatred, and they all began to collaborate together for their own demise. Her heart began to believe that she was made for the abuse.

After we made plans for her safety and departure—after we called the women's shelter and connected her to all of the needed resources, I pulled her aside and said, "I am happy that we have made all of these plans, but I know there will be a voice coming from deep inside you that will soon say . . . *The abuse ain't that bad. He doesn't beat me that much. He only leaves me stranded a bit.* When you hear that voice, I beg you not to listen. Listen to Jesus, who is beckoning you to be free from oppression." With that I sent her on her way to wait for her abuser to leave for work so that she could escape from her captor. I'd love to say she lived happily ever after. But I can't. When I saw her weeks later at church, she told me the same awful stories, yet she never really wanted to end the abuse.

Hearts get distorted. Like coral cleaved from an undersea base and robbed of its source of life, hearts get hardened. Our thoughts and emotions get twisted and torn. Our decision-making processes get off-track, and the list of things we desire gets rewritten by the wrong writers. Still, hope can be found in the redemptive community God has created and ordained.

Chapter Seven

THREE COMPELLING STORIES

KNOWING THAT HEARTS ARE EASILY DISTORTED AND KNOWING that it is essential for all to grow, God uses these two facts to create a means to usher us into a place of development and expanded capacity. Throughout Scripture, God offers us several compelling images that make the distortion unappealing and the growth attractive. In his infinite wisdom, God utilizes images of life to call us away from our dark and distorting places and into the redemptive community where our hearts are made right. God uses these images or pictures to make us hungry for being and doing more.

We Are the Temple

Within each of us is a place where God's Spirit chooses to dwell. This is the most amazing thing about God. It is not his will to be distant and removed. It is not his desire to dwell in isolation and quiet repose. Instead, it is our God's desire to dwell among his people, so much so that he chooses to allow his Spirit to dwell inside each and every one of us. In each of us an innermost shrine exists where the Spirit of God chooses to dwell. It is a shrine filled to capacity with the all-loving and relationship-craving Spirit of God. Our innermost shrine is where our spirit and God's Spirit can commune together as one. First Corinthians 6:19 says it this way: "Do you not know that your body is a temple of the Holy Spirit who is in you, whom you have from God, and that you are not your own?" (NASU).

When we commit our lives to Christ and experience the richness of baptism, the Spirit of God takes up residence inside of us. Within this interior shrine abide the sanctified thoughts, emotions, conscience, and will of Almighty God. The apostle Paul wrote to a church to let them know about this sacred space within us all. He communicated this to them in the form of a question because, as often as we are reminded of the Presence of God within us all and as many times as we have passed by this amazing concept, we often have a hard time accepting the amazing gift of God's indwelling Presence. So Paul asked this church in Corinth, "Don't you know? Haven't you owned this as truth? Haven't you embraced this picture of your higher self? God has taken up residence in you."

Now imagine what it would be like to live life from this holy place. What would life look like if we no longer reacted to life's varied situations and circumstances but instead responded to them from the place of our innermost shrine? When the hardship hits, when the obstacles arise, when the storms roll in and the trying things of life arrive, what if, instead of reacting, we respond from a place of deep and abiding intimacy with the Spirit of God? I imagine that my frustrations would settle. I imagine that my anger would subside. What if I could live my life from this innermost shrine where my spirit and God's share in a greater and greater depth of intimacy? To acknowledge the very presence of God's

Spirit inside of me is the starting place of embracing an image of my higher self. The image God wants us hungry to embrace is one where you are a carrier of the divine. Just as a bank vault is only as valuable as its holdings, so, too, is the human being. Consider your value and worth once you fully accept for a fact that within you is a shrine that serves as storehouse filled to capacity with the very Spirit of Deity. No longer is our value determined by what we own or what we have accomplished. Our worth no longer hinges on nation, borders, or military might. God says no. You are of great value and worth because deep within the depths of you is a place of communion with me.

When I accepted the reality of this innermost shrine where my spirit and the Spirit of God dwell together as a reality, I was struck with a notion. If God is in this shrine inside of me, I'd better clean some things up. When anyone of great note or prominence is coming to visit our apartment or home, we rush to dust and straighten up. We may scurry along and straighten up to hide embarrassing things we do not want seen. Or out of sheer respect you may want to make the place accommodating for your honored guest. So it was that when I learned that God's Spirit abides inside me, I wanted immediately to renovate my interior places. I wanted to renovate my innermost shrine. If the Holy Spirit of God and I are to meet there, I want to ensure that this place is clean and that no bruised emotions are hanging from the rafters. I want to make sure that no distorted thoughts are collecting in the corners like dust bunnies and long-forgotten lint. I want to make sure that my interior space is accommodating to One so majestic as the Spirit of God. So, as I sit in meditation and inhale and exhale my breath-prayer for that day, I do so in the knowledge that I am attempting to renovate the shrine where my God and I have table fellowship together. The fact that God has taken up residence in my interior place motivates me to a greater pursuit of holiness and centeredness, so that when we meet, I will no longer be concerned about the fading curtains of past indiscretions or the peeling paint of deep regrets. The only thing I want to focus on is my awareness of the fact that my Father and I are in communion. I only want to focus on being with I Am. As I accept this invitation to rest and recreate with my Father, I am embracing the image of my higher self.

Renewed in God's Rest

To motivate us, God paints pictures of our higher selves by inviting us into a time of Sabbath rest. It is interesting to note that rabbis have paid particular attention to what was said and what was not said in the creation account. Earlier we noted that after every moment of major creative activity by God, Scripture says, "There was evening and there was morning." There is deliberate mention of the opening and closing of the day. But not so with the day when God rested. Rabbis of note seem to be drawn to what was not said on God's day of Sabbath rest. They note the fact that this sentence is noticeably absent.

> Thus the heavens and the earth were completed, and
> all their hosts. By the seventh day God completed His
> work which He had done, and He rested on the seventh
> day from all His work which He had done. Then God
> blessed the seventh day and sanctified it, because in it
> He rested from all His work which God had created and
> made. (Gen. 2:1–3 NASU)

It is as if God *continues* to function from a place of Sabbath rest, not that he *ceases* to function. From that very moment, God's work is absolutely robust and absolutely effective, but it seems as if everything God does from that point on is done from a place of *shalom*—of rest.

This becomes extremely significant to us when we understand one of the key functions for Sabbath keeping. Rest is a valuable part of Sabbath keeping, of course. All of us must function with a rhythm of activity and re-creation. These moments of pause and reflection and rest give life meaning. They reinvigorate us for greater service. This time of rest makes room for celebration, reconnection with family, and the cessation of striving. Sabbath keeping also gives us renewed perspective on our role in God's divine economy. For when we "Sabbath," we no longer have our hand on the lever of life. We take our hand off what we think is the steering wheel of reality. We take our energy, time, and attention away from our work and our labor and our attempt to control what is. Then, when you rise from rest, you discover that the sun rose that day without your doing a thing. The planet kept spinning regardless of whether you were around to take note. Regardless of your participation, God made sure your business did not fall apart and your family did not sink into the dark abyss. You rise refreshed, knowing God has all of reality under control whether you, like the farmer in Mark 4, sleep at night or rise by day.

What that farmer realizes and what we come to realize when we partake in Sabbath rest is that there is an inevitability about life and life lived, because all of reality functions from a place of God's plan. God invites you to live from this same place of Sabbath rest where you work within the inevitability of God's plan. As long as you work to align your life-plan with the redemptive plan of God, you do not ever have to worry about the outcome. From this place of Sabbath rest, we know God will continue to keep the plates of our life spinning and the balls of reality in the jugglers' circle. To live from a place of Sabbath rest is to live from a place of dependency on God and his redemptive plan. This is why the Hebrews writer can say with so much confidence: "So there remains a Sabbath rest for the people of God" (Heb. 4:9 NASU).

Embracing Our Higher-Self

Our "higher self" functions from a platform of rest in God. We go to work resting in God's inevitability. We love from a place of Sabbath trust and rest. We serve from a place of re-creation and rejuvenation. The best "me" does not function from a place of exhaustion and exasperation. The picture God paints for us is an image of the higher you and the higher me living from a place of his Sabbath rest. To live from a place of Sabbath rest is to live from a place of centeredness in God's creation and creative power. It is to live from a place of balance and to live from a place of acceptance of what is instead of from a place of struggle with disappointment.

I get glimpses of that higher me in times when I unwind with these words from Psalm 45: "Be still and know that I am God." Often in moments of high stress and anxiety I run to these simple but transcendent words. I seek shelter and sanctuary in that sentence written by a shepherd king familiar with strife and striving. As I settle my breathing and make myself aware of my divine center, I say:

Be still and know that I am God.

And then I dig deeper into this Sabbath place by saying,

Be still and know that I am.

Then,

Be still and know.

And deeper in with,

Be still.

And finally,

Be.

I sink deeper and deeper into this place of Sabbath rest with God. The great contemplative and modern-day mystic Howard Thurman would call this "centering down." It is in this place of centering down that I get this glimpse of a more settled me and a more stable and mindful me. God uses that glimpse to make me want to embrace that me that lives from a place of Sabbath rest.

These biblical images of my higher nature are set before me in the hope that they will make me hungry for growth and development. The Bible attempts to stoke the furnace of my desire to fuel in me a burning desire to do better and to be better. All of this motivates me to seek the best possible ways to fashion experiences for everyone in which they can naturally bump into things that make them grow.

This leads to the question: *What are the common traits that must be available in the life of the believer that will allow those opportunities to take root in our lives and thereby allow God to grow us as he desires?*

Join me as we journey through the answers I found—truths that make up the first seven lessons of faith.

Part 2

THE SEVEN LESSONS

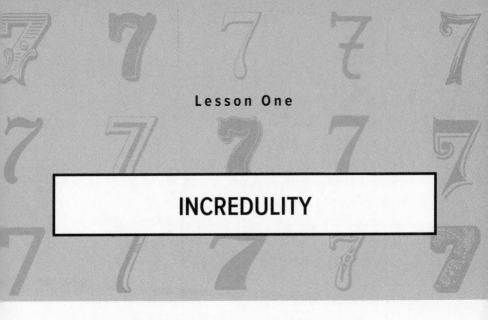

INCREDULITY

*Your level of growth is commensurate with
your level of unrest with the status quo.*

A LITTLE FISSURE BREAKS INTO OUR REALITY WHEN DISTRUST arises. When truthfulness is called into question, something happens in the air around us. A social contract is broken. A balance is set off-kilter. When incredulity spreads, something deep and thick occurs in all of us.

Unfortunately distrust runs rampant these days. In this age we seldom assume that a person is telling the truth. I think the prevailing assumption is that everyone in some way is telling a lie. Incredulity is a word that characterizes much of how we deal with one another in life, in love, and in discourse. I long for the day when a person's word meant something, when deals were made with two people looking each other in the eye and firmly shaking hands. I'm so incredulous at this point that I wonder if that time ever really existed, or if it was a myth offered by others in the hope they could use that naïveté against the believer of that myth at a later time. Incredulity is prevalent, but it is not always bad. Sometimes we need to be suspicious. At times, we need to question.

It was one of those life-changing days in graduate school, and I did not even know it. We sat in a circle around a huge conference table, hanging on to every word of our professor. We were discussing historic fallacies in ages past. Then it finally clicked for me. I had been so shackled and brainwashed by my upbringing in the racial south that I couldn't help my ignorance. Have you ever had moments like that when you begin thinking so differently, when the light bulb goes off so brightly, that truth comes flooding in with such force that the words you are thinking become the words you are actually saying without your realizing you are saying them out loud? Perhaps to your detriment?

Until that moment I couldn't believe that researchers falsify their findings. In my naive and brainwashed state, I figured that no one intentionally would skew the research. I couldn't fathom people manipulating the data. Before I knew it, I blurted out, "You mean to tell me people can get away with writing lies in these books?" My professor, who was known to be one of the most crotchety curmudgeons on staff, had mercy on me that day and said, "Welcome to graduate school, Mr. Wilson!" as if to say, "Thank you for joining us finally in the realization that we need to question the things we are given to believe."

One of the most important things we must question is the status quo. We must boldly and bravely look at the effectiveness of the way things currently are. There must be an outright incredulity of the prevailing norms. This takes us to our first lesson of faith: incredulity. Here, we learn,

> *Your level of growth is commensurate with your level of unrest with the status quo.*

Hebrews 11:8–10 says this about the patriarch Abraham:

> By faith Abraham, when called to go to a place he would later receive as his inheritance, obeyed and went, even though he did not know where he was going. By faith he made his home in the promised land like a stranger in a foreign country; he lived in tents, as did Isaac and Jacob, who were heirs with him of the same promise. For he was looking forward to the city with foundations, whose architect and builder is God.

Abraham was called from his prevailing norm to a new reality. He was invited into a search for a new status.

My first years of ministry were absolutely a diving into the great unknown. Let me share an experience I recorded in a journal during a tense moment in that period of my ministry:

> A conversation at the Artisan Coffee House turned dramatic and a student in a rant stood up yelling about how miserable her life was . . .
>
> As she quick-step traipsed away, in almost resignation I said a breath-prayer, maybe for her to hear, "I praise God you're disquieted."

Soul (with all of the anger she could muster, eyes narrowed and focused to the size of the head of a pin): What did you say?
Friend: I praise God you are disquieted.
Soul: I'm questioning everything I ever believed, and you're sitting there praising God for it?
Friend: Don't you think it's about time that you did? I mean, how long were you going to hinge your life on things you had never questioned? Yeah, (as I become

more convinced of God's presence in this conflict)
frankly, I do praise God you are unsettled.

Now this is that moment, that liminal time and space where anything can happen. She's standing five feet away from the coffeehouse door and five feet away from my table. This is threshold. This is in-betweeness. I couldn't pray. I could not breathe. Anything could happen. Storm out, spit on me, cry, make a scene, anything. Listen to her feet, man. That will probably be the first thing to move, the first to give a clue of what's to come. Arches lower to the ground right behind the ball of the foot. Heels touched down. Weight resting. Shift. She sits.

> *Friend:* God has never intended you to be satisfied with
> your spiritual condition. He implanted restlessness
> in your make-up, embedded it in your spiritual DNA,
> so to speak. I mean, you think so much of your life
> is happenstance or your lot is different than other
> people's lot. It ain't. It just isn't. We all have restlessness
> for completeness. You know this from life, right? A
> "lack of" produces a "want for." Doesn't it? It's that way
> everywhere you look. A hungry man wants what?
> *Soul:* Food.
> *Friend:* Right! A homeless man needs what?
> *Soul:* A home.
> *Friend:* Yep, and a poor man wants for what?
> *Soul:* Money.
> *Friend:* See, a "lack of" produces a "want for" or "need
> for." What if there was some one . . . better yet, some
> being that was wise enough to take that dynamic and
> use it for his people's good. God craves for you to be
> complete. He has determined for you to be complete.

He wants you to be complete and whole because he is complete and whole. What Father doesn't want his kids to look and act like him? But, but, but, this some-being is also wise enough to know other human conditions. Like the fact that we for the most part are lazy. We want things given to us, and if we strive for anything, we will move first to the path of least resistance. Being whole is not for the lazy and will not be found by taking any path marked "least resistance." So how does he get us off our duffs? By utilizing the lack of/want for. Make them lack it to fuel a want for it. He is so masterful at this. It's amazing.

As I watched her, I thought: I might need to pull up on the enthusiasm. I might be scaring her away as I foam at the mouth out of sheer exaltation of God's greatness. Something in my gut told me this was true. Then a retired philosophy professor showed me that this is true and later a minister showed me this in the Bible. Ecclesiastes 3:11 . . . It's right there. God implanted eternity in our hearts. They showed me, and both times I started foaming at the mouth. Here I go again.

Friend: Think about it this way. At the very moment God created the night and day, the moment he made the sun to rise and set, people started wanting to find eternity. See with the rising and setting of the sun we got a measure of time. There was a time when there wasn't time. As a matter of fact, there is going to be a time again when there won't be any time. But, man, at the point when people start to measure out time, you can see that some people live many risings and settings of the sun and others only a few. Or like they say in those old westerns—where they put the Native Americans out there looking and sounding all crazy—some people live many moons and others not so many. With the marking of time comes the news that we are finite creatures who lack longevity or, more to the point, eternity. We are not whole; we lack the ability to last. Then we want it. Got to have it. A lack of produces a want for. Then God's got you just where he wants you. You become restless because you become a craver for eternal life. Or you become restless because you know there is a void that must be filled. What do you do with the void? Will you continue to curse the rising and setting sun because it makes you aware of your mortality, or are you going to do something about becoming immortal? Do you lack or do you do something about fulfilling the want? Do you curse the void or do something about filling it?

Soul: I don't have any voids in my life. I have a life. I have a job. I have a family that loves me. I'm doing great in most every aspect of my life.

Friend: Then why are you yelling at me?

Soul: Because you are so convinced that something is wrong with me, and you think you know me but you don't.

Friend: I don't think I know you. I know myself, and I'm speaking out of my own sense of frustration and brokenness. But if I'm wrong, I'm wrong. You don't have a void in your life that needs to be filled. You don't crave more.

*Silence
A lot of silence
A lot more silence.*

Friend: You want something to drink?
Soul: For me to have a void, I would have to feel some
emptiness. I don't.
Friend: Voids are vacuums. They get filled, or they
remain in a state of process where they are getting filled.
So most of the time we don't feel them because we are
so busy filling them. What I was getting at is beginning
to look at what we fill them with. College, boyfriend,
family, job.

My conversation with that student didn't end when my journal
entry did. Here's what followed:

We have to get away from being cool with the way things are.
We have to be disquieted; we have to be uncomfortable. We have to
be willing to make a break with the status quo. Business-as-usual
does not move us deeper into relationship with Christ. Things are
not supposed to be good enough or all right. We are to have life
and have it to the full.

You are getting something out of stagnation. You like it. Not
the stagnation—we all hate stagnation. We can smell the festering
in our lives. I'm not suggesting you like the stagnation, but you
like whatever you get out of the stagnation.

What could I possibly get out of it that I would like?

I don't know. It could be any number of things. It could be that
you get the comfort of knowing you're okay. Because to come to
terms with understanding that none of us are okay is disquieting.
We can exert energy toward other things instead of the things
that really matter. I can focus my attention on a job and making
money, focus on fun and the accumulation of stuff. Now I'm just

like everyone else, and isn't that what we want? We want to belong. Even if it is a rat-race that we belong to, we belong.

So you're saying I shouldn't have any of those things. See, that's the thing about faith that I cannot tolerate. This idea of not having fun or having anything. There is nothing wrong with accomplishing things. I'm in college now busting my hump trying to get a degree so that I can help people. So are you saying I shouldn't be devoting my attention to that? Or shouldn't have a nice car or a nice place to live?

I never said you shouldn't have those. I'm talking about the payoff we get for status-quo living. The payoff that we receive by staying tuned into the rhythms of this world, the droning cadence of stagnation. We get something out of it or we wouldn't stay that way. Payoff is a big thing in our life and motivations. Having cars and homes and nice stuff is fine. I wouldn't make it a focus, but that's fine. But if we want real life and the Kingdom living that our hearts crave, we have to acknowledge that we get something out of doing nothing. If we defuse the payoff, we are able to respond to our sense of dissatisfaction and move to real living.

See, we are tabernacle people. We have a tabernacle God so we are tabernacle people. Do you remember what a tabernacle is?

Yeah, wasn't it a tent or something that those people used in the Old Testament?

Yep, and what was in this tent?

God, right? God was in this tent, and Moses would go talk to him there, right?

Yeah, you remember. See God wanted to have an intimate relationship with his chosen people, the Jewish nation, the children of Israel. So God says to them, "I'm going to pitch my tent in your midst. I want to be with you." The people were living in tents, and God's tent, his tabernacle, was among their tents. For a long time they were a nomadic group. These people and their God moved from place to place, looking for a better place to stay. But God lets us know, "I'm not bound to a church building or temple. I move around. I am everywhere, and all of me is everywhere at the same time." God preferred the tabernacle because it is closer to the picture of who he really is: a God that is not bound to one place. Because we are his children, the idea is to act like him. If God is not bound to one spot, neither are we. We are tabernacle people, always moving, and, ideally always progressing to a better place. In order to begin moving to that special place, we have to be willing to take up our tent and move. We have to be dissatisfied with the space we are currently in to be willing to find something better. We are tabernacle people.

Look, you don't have to be stuck. I'm not trying to put that on you. You obviously are a driven young lady who has a lot going for her. I'm merely saying that until you are convinced that there is something better out there than the payoff that you get now, you will not move.

I continued with this student by asking her the same question I will ask you to consider: *What do you do with the void?* What are some of the things people can do to address the voids in their lives? Will you continue to curse the rising and setting sun because it makes you aware of your mortality, or are you going to do something about becoming immortal? Do you lack, or do you do something about fulfilling the want? Do you curse the void or do something about filling it? Whatever you do, you have to mean to do it.

INTENTIONALITY

*Your level of growth is commensurate
with your level of commitment.*

THREE DECADES AFTER FINISHING THE CEILING OF THE SISTINE Chapel, Michelangelo returns to this same sacred space to begin work on a fresco. I could only imagine the joints of his fingers constricting and the small of his back tightening as he remembers the laborious work that took place in that space those many years ago. This next work is to span the entire wall behind the altar of the massive chapel. The painting is to depict the second coming of Jesus Christ and the apocalypse. Michelangelo begins seeing the radiant Christ in the middle of the composition, surrounded by the saints from all ages. All around them are the souls ascending to their reward or descending into the hands of waiting tormentors who drag them to their demise. This painting would take eight years to complete. But before it can be finished, the artist painstakingly produces over two thousand sketches and renderings just to get it right. Without a doubt Michelangelo got it right. "The Last Judgment" is massive in scale, scope, and sensibility. It is considered one of the twelve master paintings of the age. Why? Because the artist intended it to be so. There is power in intentionality.

It must be reiterated over and over again that God is the source of our growth in faith and spiritual development. He uses a variety of means to mold us and shape us into the image of Christ. It also must be repeatedly confirmed that we have a role to play as well if this growth process is to take place. Our role is to place ourselves consistently in the proper trajectory for God to do what he ultimately intends to do with us all. Growth in faith and spiritual development will not occur by happenstance or coincidence, nor will it happen by luck or fluke. We must aim to place ourselves full body into the flow of God's transcendent process. This takes us to the second lesson of faith: intentionality. This second lesson states,

> *Your level of growth is commensurate*
> *with your level of commitment.*

This is confirmed by the ever-direct, Quaker author William Law. In his book *A Serious Call to a Devout and Holy Life*, Law states, "Now if you will stop here and ask yourself why you are not as pious as the primitive Christians were, your own heart will tell you that it is neither through ignorance nor inability, but purely because you never thoroughly intended it." The only thing we can say to that is ouch! It cuts us at the core of who we are. His words strike a chord within us that is painful to pluck and at the same time dissonant to the ear. If we were Judgment-day honest, we would have to admit that there is a ring of truth to this. Regardless of what happens during our day, we will always make time for food, maybe for a rest, for making love to our spouse, or for paying some attention to our work, but our spiritual life sometimes wanes from lack of intention. This happens, although our soul's self knows implicitly that there is power in intentionality.

Joshua: An Example of Intentionality

"But as for me and my house, we will serve the Lord." This is a statement redolent with intentionality. It is bold in its phrasing and courageous in its positioning. It's the aggressive claim of a man who truly understood the power of intentionality. The man who made this statement was named Joshua, and intentionality shaped the man Joshua became.

We first encounter Joshua when he was the servant of Moses. Joshua served as his aide and helper as Moses attempted to move the children of Israel from the status of slaves to full citizens of a Kingdom life. As we observe how Joshua served, we see moment after moment of intentionality. In Exodus 33:11 we see this picture of the man: "The LORD would speak to Moses face to face, as a man speaks with his friend. Then Moses would return to the camp, but his young aide Joshua son of Nun did not leave the tent." While Moses would leave the Presence of the Lord to bring a fresh word to a weary people, Joshua would stay. Joshua, full of resolve and awareness, held vigil at the tent of meeting, as if to say, "Moses if you must go, please do so. I have to stay, because if the Lord is present, I will be here to listen. If the Lord speaks, we do not want to miss it. There may be a message of encouragement, or God may provide guidance of some kind. Whatever it may be, we don't want to miss a word of it." Joshua's intent was to be fully present for the Lord and for Moses.

Upon their arrival at the Promised Land, Joshua was sent, along with eleven others, to spy out the land. He was sent on a reconnaissance mission to see if the land was as good as it was reported to be, to find out about the land and what it had to offer. Yet after spying out the land and returning to offer their report, several of the men who went with Joshua offered more than a scouting report. After letting everyone know that the land indeed was good, they degenerated into cowardly comments and fearful statements. "Sure the land is great, but we can't go there," they warned. "There are giants in the land, and they have fortified cities. Moses, it can't be done. Don't make us go back there!"

This was the word of the majority of the spies who went forth, but not of Joshua and his friend Caleb. They believed in the covenant promise. They believed in the possibility of a gracious God working on behalf of his chosen people. So with great faith and forethought Joshua counseled the people:

> The land we passed through and explored is exceedingly good. If the LORD is pleased with us, he will lead us into that land, a land flowing with milk and honey, and will give it to us. Only do not rebel against the LORD. And do not be afraid of the people of the land, because we will swallow them up. Their protection is gone, but the LORD is with us. Do not be afraid of them. (Num. 14:7–9)

There is unrelenting power in intentionality. This is what Joshua, many years later, attempts to pass on to the next generation of God-followers now in the Promised Land. Joshua takes the people of God through a process of refining their level of intentionality. He takes them through a moment of re-covenanting with God.

What I love about this moment is how Joshua utilizes the power of space. Joshua knows that space is significant. Space and location can serve as a container of memory and meaning. One only has to ponder briefly about a space or place where something of great importance took place in their lives. Where is that for you? Was it a classroom where you met your first best friend? Is it a restaurant where you knew you had truly fallen in love? Where is it for you? If you can conceive of the place, you have to admit that in this space there is meaning. Space is redolent with a sense of importance. A pilgrimage to such a place causes stories to be retold. Memories, once dormant, come flooding back to mind, and feelings become fresh in your heart. This is what Joshua taps into as he takes the children of Israel to a place called Shechem.

Shechem is where God fully commits to Abraham, and where Abraham fully commits to God. Shechem is where Jacob raises an altar to God after God spares him from his brother Esau's wrath. Shechem is where Jacob makes his family rid themselves of foreign gods and idols and recommit to God. Now, as an old man, Joshua gathers everyone up in Shechem to teach them about intentionality.

> Joshua said to all the people, "This is what the Lord, the God of Israel, says: 'Long ago your forefathers, including Terah the father of Abraham and Nahor, lived beyond the River and worshiped other gods. But I took your father Abraham from the land beyond the River and led him throughout Canaan and gave him many descendants. I gave him Isaac, and to Isaac I gave Jacob and Esau. I assigned the hill country of Seir to Esau, but Jacob and his sons went down to Egypt.
>
> "Then I sent Moses and Aaron, and I afflicted the Egyptians by what I did there, and I brought you out. When I brought your fathers out of Egypt, you came to the sea, and the Egyptians pursued them with chariots and horsemen as far as the Red Sea. But they cried to the Lord for help, and he put darkness between you and the Egyptians; he brought the sea over them and covered them. You saw with your own eyes what I did

to the Egyptians. Then you lived in the desert for a long time.

"I brought you to the land of the Amorites who lived east of the Jordan. They fought against you, but I gave them into your hands. I destroyed them from before you, and you took possession of their land. When Balak son of Zippor, the king of Moab, prepared to fight against Israel, he sent for Balaam son of Beor to put a curse on you. But I would not listen to Balaam, so he blessed you again and again, and I delivered you out of his hand.

"Then you crossed the Jordan and came to Jericho. The citizens of Jericho fought against you, as did also the Amorites, Perizzites, Canaanites, Hittites, Girgashites, Hivites, and Jebusites, but I gave them into your hands. I sent the hornet ahead of you, which drove them out before you—also the two Amorite kings. You did not do it with your own sword and bow. So I gave you a land on which you did not toil and cities you did not build; and you live in them and eat from vineyards and olive groves that you did not plant." (Josh. 24:2–13)

In this process of re-covenanting for the purpose of intentionality, Joshua uses space as a vehicle for the production of meaning as well as a container of values that need to be passed on. Then Joshua spends time rehearsing this instructive, life-shaping narrative. Joshua rehearses. He literally takes them through a process where they re-hear what he must say. Joshua re-says in their hearing a narrative or story that is to become how they see their world and how they are to function in reality. He rehearses this essential narrative, re-telling the story of God's righteousness and covenant faithfulness. He tells how their nation survived, and he stresses the fact that their survival was not because of their behavior, but in spite of it.

After proclaiming in their hearing the story of their survival, Joshua commands them:

> Now fear the Lord and serve him with all faithful-
> ness. Throw away the gods your forefathers worshiped
> beyond the River and in Egypt, and serve the LORD.
> But if serving the LORD seems undesirable to you, then
> choose for yourselves this day whom you will serve,
> whether the gods your forefathers served beyond the
> River, or the gods of the Amorites, in whose land you
> are living. But as for me and my household, we will
> serve the LORD. (Josh. 24:14–15)

Joshua clarifies to the children of Israel the only two options provided for them that day. The choices then, as for us today, remain these: serve God or the lesser things of the past. These were their choices, just as they are our choices today. Joshua, not out of arrogance or pride, emphatically states what his plans are in this regard. He and all of his family choose God.

The fact that Joshua states his intent is so important. In a time of hedging bets, moral ambiguity, and waffling, men and women need to proclaim their decisions before the world and set examples of intentionality. The growth of faith is not an easy thing. Moving into places of mystery and unknown in order to be stretched and expanded is not something to be taken lightly. For many of us, it is treacherous terrain to tread. We often need a forerunner or an example speaking words of intentionality just to make the journey and commitment make sense. That is what Joshua, the consummate leader of his people, is attempting to do. Joshua wants to let the people he loves and leads have an example of intentionality for the purpose of promoting intentionality in them. So the clarion call sounds forth from Joshua: "As for me and my house, we will serve the Lord."

Then, to complete this process of re-covenanting, Joshua does something remarkable. He recites their commitments to God and God's commitments to them before a rock. That rock becomes a witness to their exercise in intentionality. Much like the Celtic wedding tradition of the oathing stone where the couple pledges their love to one another with their hands clutching or their feet resting on a rock, Joshua makes a pledge to God for his people with a stone serving as witness. This rock stands as a stalwart reminder of the commitments they make that day to God. So, as they venture in and out of the Promised Land, there will be a lasting memorial, a reminder of their intentional commitment to God and to the things of God.

> On that day Joshua made a covenant for the people,
> and there at Shechem he drew up for them decrees and
> laws. And Joshua recorded these things in the Book of
> the Law of God. Then he took a large stone and set it
> up there under the oak near the holy place of the LORD.
> "See!" he said to all the people. "This stone will be a
> witness against us. It has heard all the words the LORD
> has said to us. It will be a witness against you if you are
> untrue to your God." (Josh. 24:25–27)

Memory plays such an important role in intentionality and spiritual formation. It has always played a vital role in faith. When Jesus invites his followers to table fellowship, he calls them to eat the bread and drink from the cup and to do it in remembrance of him. The children of Israel, once they had crossed the Jordan River, placed twelve stones on a mound to remember how God delivered them. The prayer shawls worn by rabbis hung low with tassels to remind them of the commands they were to live by and proclaim.

Even circumcision served Hebrew men as a constant reminder of sacrifice and commitment to God.

Marked by the Lord

I think one of the most beautiful functions of the Holy Spirit of God is that of a seal. Anytime a merchant from a faraway land purchased an item to take back with him, that item would be marked with a seal. Sometimes this seal was an image from a signet ring stamped in wax. In other cases, that seal was just a unique and distinctive mark. Certain qualities were affirmed and characteristics assumed about anything that held the purchaser's specific seal. When an item was marked with a seal, the seller and purchaser affirmed the authenticity of the item sealed. What was sealed was, in fact, what it was claimed to be. Also whatever was sealed was assumed to be worth the purchase price. Whatever held the purchaser's seal was definitely going home with the purchaser. So, while the purchaser might journey on to other distant lands and ports of call, and while he might be delayed by other concerns or business dealings; upon his return, the mark of his seal reminded him of any items that were to go home with him. This is what Paul is saying to us when he writes that God has sealed us and given us the Spirit in our hearts as a pledge (2 Cor. 1:22). Or when he tells us, "Do not grieve the Holy Spirit of God, with whom you were sealed for the day of redemption" (Eph. 4:30).

As those who have intentionally committed our lives to Christ, we have been purchased by Christ. The cost he paid for us was his blood shed for us on the cross. This seal says to us and to him, "Those under this seal are authenticated as followers." Our value and worthwhileness have been raised due to the exorbitant cost paid for us. Without a doubt, when Christ returns and decides to go home, those with his seal are going home with him. The seal of the Holy Spirit is a reminder to the purchaser that we are truly his.

As those who have been purchased, this seal is even more important to us today, for it is a reminder of who we are, of the cost paid for us, and of the trajectory of our aim—which is home. As a result, in all of this, memory becomes an important factor to our faith.

This is especially true when it comes to intentionality, because if we are to be intentional, we must always remember where our intentions and commitments lie. If faithfulness does not stand in the forefront of our minds by default, we will waver in our constancy. If growth does not remain a hallmark of our day, we may settle for malaise. If Christlikeness is not remembered as being tantamount to our being-ness, we may begin functioning as others function and lagging as others lag. So the Joshua saga teaches us the significance of memory as an integral part of intentionality.

I love the advice the father of the great tenor Luciano Pavarotti gave him. Pavarotti said in an interview,

> When I was a boy, my father, a baker, introduced me to the wonders of song. He urged me to work very hard to develop my voice. Arrigo Pola, a professional tenor in my hometown of Modena, Italy, took me as a pupil. I also enrolled in a teachers' college. On graduating, I asked my father, "Shall I be a teacher or a singer?" "Luciano," my father replied, "if you try to sit on two chairs, you will fall between them. For life, you must choose one chair."
>
> I chose one. It took seven years of study and frustration before I made my first professional appearance. It took another seven to reach the Metropolitan Opera. And now I think that whether it's laying bricks, writing a book, whatever we choose, we should give ourselves to it. Commitment, that's the key. Choose one chair.

This is the power displayed in Jesus Christ while he was here on Earth to carry out the redemptive plan of his Father. That was his one chair. One who carefully examines the dynamics at play in Jesus's earthly ministry will find a distinct moment when Jesus really leans into the inevitability of his sacrifice on the cross. Luke 9:51 says, "As the time approached for him to be taken up to heaven, Jesus resolutely set out for Jerusalem."

Intentionality is a resolute turning. Intentionality is a turning away from distraction and indecision to a purposefulness that says, "God's will is going to get done through me instead of in spite of me. His redemptive plan will be carried out because of me and not regardless of me." Intentionality is a resolute turning that works inside the belief that nothing will stop God's irresistible outpouring of justice on the world.

When I entered into a compound north of Lusaka in Zambia, I was faced with the testing of this belief. This desolate squatters' village confirmed the fact that there is always a subfloor to poverty. There is always poorer. There is always greater lack. Two students of mine were teaching in this caldron of want. I was actually riding shotgun with the gentleman who was gracious enough to drive them, but, because the sun was going down and these brave young men were preaching in an area littered with makeshift taverns that fed the despair of the hurting with homemade liquor, I was asked to travel with him to extract the students. As we arrived at the location, I was made acutely aware of two things. These men were preaching in one of the bars, and in such a setting it pays to be a six-foot-two, two hundred sixty-pound servant of God.

As the inhabitants of the surrounding bars poured out from their stupor to see who this was invading their space, we found our way into a tavern-turned-sanctuary. Huddled into this cramped place were the hurting, the broken, children, leaping on the floor or strapped to their mothers' backs by stained but sturdy sashes. All of them were listening for some word of hope, promise, or possibility. These two students of mine, Zambian-born and craving an outpouring of the Kingdom where they lived, were shouting with raised hands into a sound system held together by bailing wire, duct tape, and prayer. They saw me enter and, with far too much deference, stopped what they were doing to introduce me to their ailing flock and to suggest that someday there might be a chance for me to speak a word from God to them.

Immediately my mind began looking for any word or any sense of hope I could possibly provide for these hurting people if the chance were to occur. Was there a word of hope for them? Really? Was there a word of hope for those in the midst of such utter poverty? This was not the type of poverty we have in the West, where there is a chance that table scraps might fall from the feasting table of the haves to assuage the hunger of the have-nots. Was there a word for those in the kind of poverty that can't anticipate scraps because there is no table?

My sense of intentionality was tested in that tavern, and the only thing I had to hold on to in that moment was the resolute turning that I had made years before—the same conviction that functions inside many believers—that justice will reach people like this as well. God's righteousness will reach them, even if manmade handouts fall far short. Whether we deem it necessary or possible to reach out to raise the dignity of the hapless few huddled tightly in a similar bar in some far-flung corner of the world, God deems it so. Based on this belief, we carry out intentional behaviors day in and day out. We can participate in some large or small way if we choose to. If we, in fact, want to grow to participate in this inevitable outpouring of God's Kingdom to the most hurting and to the least blessed, then there must be on our part a resolute turning in keeping with intentionality.

The Power of Intentionality

Intentionality certainly heightens awareness. All of us have an ardent need to gain a sense of spiritual acuity. Spiritual acuity is a clarified vision of what is and of what is eternal. While we may be able to see the transient and the temporary or those things that are considered "but a vapor," it is of utmost importance that we have a clarified vision of what lasts beyond the temporal. I am convinced this is one of the reasons we see so many miraculous healings of sight all through the Bible. Jesus is trying to key us in on the importance of truly being able to see. He intentionally aids in this process.

At one time in my life I felt it was an absolute need to drive cars that were peculiar or different—something that had an appeal to it because it was a car not typically seen in the towns I lived in. Of course, this speaks to the folly of youth and maybe of a need for greater growth in esteem. Okay, let's go with this as not a maybe, but a definite. But I would hunt. I would hunt for that one vehicle nobody else had. Once it was the Land Rover. Found it. Bought it. Drove it. Soon regretted the whole proposition. What I found interesting was that prior to my purchase of the vehicle, I never saw one in the small town where I lived and worked, but after driving it one day, I noticed fifteen of them. Did a dealer all of a sudden decide to flood the market of my small town with Land Rovers to thwart my plan for uniqueness? Certainly not! Instead, as I soon realized, that purchase made me keenly aware of what I was previously blind to. My eyes became acutely aware of the vehicle I just purchased. Owning one provided greater clarity of vision that formerly was not there. Intentionality works in the same way.

Unawareness is functioning from a place of such distractedness that the obvious becomes the unobtrusive. But, when I intend to see something, it becomes the very thing I see. If I'm predisposed to seeing scarcity, this is what I see all around me. It works the same if

I intend to see abundance; I see it everywhere. If I am predisposed to encountering obstacles, this is what I perceive all about me. Yet, if I intend to see opportunity, this is what becomes the hallmark of my environment. If I am predisposed to see hatred and bitterness, I see it everywhere. When with dogged insistence I choose to see, despite the world's sick urgings, the world bathed in the overflow of compassion and love emanating from the very throne of God, this is what I see more than anything else. For me to see this, I must utilize intentionality to develop greater spiritual acuity.

As I study faith and spiritual growth from a variety of traditions, I find three contemplative assumptions powerfully present when people in all ages discuss intentionality. Those three assumptions are:

1. Where I place my intention is where I place my attention.
2. Intentionality expands capacity.
3. Where you place your attention impacts your condition.

We certainly see all three of these assumptions at play in the life of one of the first Christ-followers named Peter. We notice this amazingly curious moment in Matthew 14:

> Immediately Jesus made the disciples get into the boat and go on ahead of him to the other side, while he dismissed the crowd. After he had dismissed them, he went up on a mountainside by himself to pray. When evening came, he was there alone, but the boat was already a considerable distance from land, buffeted by the waves because the wind was against it.
>
> During the fourth watch of the night Jesus went out to them, walking on the lake. When the disciples saw him walking on the lake, they were terrified. "It's a ghost," they said, and cried out in fear.

But Jesus immediately said to them: "Take courage!
It is I. Don't be afraid." "Lord, if it's you," Peter replied,
"tell me to come to you on the water." (14:22–28)

Peter calls Jesus Lord, and don't believe for a moment that he says this out of obligation, deference, or cordiality. He speaks out of intentionality. In effect, Peter says, "Jesus, I call you Lord, because I believe this is who you are. I am fully committed to this notion of your Lordship. So I turn all of my attention toward you, because where I place my intentions is where I place my attention. So I place my attention on your Lordship right now!"

Peter's desire is to intend to confirm the Lordship of Jesus Christ. The outcome of that attempt is expanded capacity on Peter's part. For, in response to Peter's request, Jesus says, "Come."

Peter comes. He climbs out of the boat and places a tentative foot on the unstable and precarious waves. Despite reason and despite Peter's vast base of knowledge as a fisherman to confirm his fears, he comes. Through intentionality, the space where Peter's feet can tread is greatly expanded. Beyond solid ground and manmade structures, Peter's capacity to tread is expanded to include water and waves at the very moment Jesus says, "Come." Intentionality expands capacity.

What we also find at play in this seminal moment of Peter's life is the last contemplative assumption in relation to intentionality: where I place my intention impacts my condition. Notice what happens next in this incredible moment of intentionality. Matthew sees this scene: "Then Peter got down out of the boat, walked on the water and came toward Jesus. But when he saw the wind, he was afraid and, beginning to sink, cried out." When Peter switches his intended focus away from the confirmation of the Lordship of Jesus Christ and begins to concentrate on the raging winds, his condition changes, because what we place our attention on becomes the object that has greater sway on our condition. Instead of allowing the focus on Jesus to expand his capacity, now the winds become the greater source of influence on Peter's condition, and at once he begins to sink. That is, until Peter reestablishes his attention on the Lordship of Jesus Christ and he cries: "Lord, save me!" Immediately Jesus reaches out his hand and catches Peter. "You of little faith," Jesus says, "why did you doubt?" And when they climb into the boat, the wind dies down (Matt. 14:29–32).

Peter's condition is gravely impacted by where he places his attention. The same is true for us all. If we place our attention on those things that bring us down, this shift of focus saps our energy, chips away at our faith, and, like Peter, we find ourselves drowning. The very moment we fix our eyes on those things that enliven us and offer consolation, our condition immediately changes.

When Our Intentionality Wavers

Intentionality and commitment can be strengthened.

All is not lost if we waver in intentionality. This wavering can come after long bouts of confusion and wandering. It can come about by just living life itself. Life has a way of battering us like waves against gradually eroding cliffs. We may not notice the consequences of the unrelenting tide. In some cases it may be only after years of living that you realize that the self you once knew has been abraded. The commitments you once had have been replaced with the tepid notion of going along and getting along. The tasks of the day seem to have eclipsed the goals those tasks were meant to fulfill. But long-neglected intentionality can be regained.

The key is to commit to the notion that we can be fully human. When God created humanity, he declared that this life he made is not just good, but very good. He saw in his creation the possibility of much good. As a matter of fact, Jesus sees one human soul as having greater worth than gaining the whole world. The problem with humanity is that so many of us live so far below the potential of being fully human. Whether because of sin or because we exist in toxic environments for way too long, the human soul begins to atrophy. The human spirit finds itself in disrepair and decay. If we stay in intentional sin long enough or we find ourselves dwelling in toxic environments of abuse or neglect, we become less and less human and certainly less humane.

How wonderful that Jesus comes bursting on the scene to show us how to be fully human. He invites us into a relationship where the human spirit is revived and the human soul reshaped. Jesus comes as exemplar, forerunner, and friend to usher us into opportunity after opportunity to become fully human. With Christ there is forgiveness of sin. There is freedom from the oppression of toxic environments. There is even restoration of the human heart to such a degree that capacity is expanded and intentionality once lost is regained.

There is this wonderful acting exercise directors use with actors. The aim is for authentic emotions, reactions, and responses, but often actors feel so alienated from the roles they play that the emotional depth is hard to achieve. That is, until the director leads them in an exercise of discovering the "given circumstances" or "givens," as they are often called. The given circumstances are the actual events that are unfolding in the character's life. These circumstances are as varied as the scope and breadth of theater itself.

- A father struggles to find meaning in his life as he faces the regrets of his past.
- A woman attempts to find a place in a world where she no longer fits.
- A son is torn between cowardice and avenging his father's murder.

The background of these "givens" is found in the script but fleshed out by the actor's imagination. The director asks, "What would it feel like to actually live in this circumstance?" The actor considers this. What would the weight of that burden feel like? Gradually, the character's emotional landscape is mapped out by traveling through the character's situations. Once the twists, turns, inclines, and roads are explored, the only reasonable response is an authentic portrayal.

I long for the day when all Christians explore the given circumstances of their walk with Christ—to sit with the weight of so lavish a grace they have been given, to really grasp the scope of history, past, present, and future where their lives have been woven. I wish each of us could actually grasp the significance of bringing justice to those who have been denied this right, or understand the profound joy of hearing the words, "Your sins are forgiven." If we truly grasped the "givens" of faith, the only reasonable response will be commitment and intentionality. And, with this newfound sense of purpose, we can find ourselves moving into deeper and deeper depths of growth in our faith.

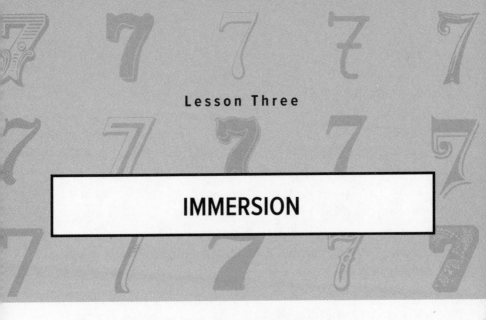

IMMERSION

Your growth is commensurate with
your depth of exposure.

I T'S SO INTERESTING THAT I PREACH WITH PASSION; I TEACH WITH passion; I live with a sense of passion. However, the most impor- tant moment of my spiritual life, my baptism, was not a moment of passion but one of settled and centered reason. I was sitting in a church service the Sunday after a series of intense discussions with my now wife but then fiancée, about faith, and then a song was sung. In tones more chanted than sung, the words rang out,

> *Oh, I want to see him,*
> *look upon his face,*
> *there to sing forever of his grace.*
> *On the streets of glory let me lift my voice,*
> *All my cares are past,*

I'm home at last,
Ever to rejoice.

The reasoned thought became, yes, I want to see Jesus. Much like Shakespeare's Othello, I demanded "ocular proof"! Since I was a child, I had sensed his presence. Since I was a child, I'd heard his name extolled. Yes, I wanted to see him. I had to. It was not good enough to hear of his saving grace. No! It was not enough to know he died for my sin. When all was said and done, it seemed reasonable to me to do whatever it took to lay my eyes on Jesus. So I was immersed; I was submerged; I was buried in water and ushered into a life of re-creation with Christ. I was birthed anew through the matrix of water. Little did I know that instead of baptism becoming a means for me to see Jesus in the sweet by and by, it became a means for me to see his hand functioning in my life in the rough and rugged here-and-now.

Baptism Stories

I have to admit I am a sucker for a good baptism story. To hear of baptisms and to witness them always gives me a thrill and takes me back to the moment of my own immersion. These are powerful moments in the life of a believer and for the life of a church. I have seen the power of God's hand through the power of baptism.

I remember the second week of my first preaching ministry at a church. One of the church leaders came to me with eyes the size of silver dollars, saying, "A visitor wants to get baptized." I could tell by the look on her face that she was not excited by the baptism but was concerned about the visitor who was making the request. I sat with the visitor, who told me that she struggled with multiple personality disorder and that most of her multiple personalities had been baptized at one time or another, but now she was actually in her right state of mind. Because of this she wanted to get baptized immediately before one of her personalities took over. She wanted to know if I would I be willing to do it that very minute.

What does one do in moments like that? The only thing I knew to do was to pray. And pray hard! So I prayed this prayer of integration over her. Knowing that so much of what baptism is about is identity and solidifying an integrated identity in Christ Jesus, I prayed for her integration. I prayed that every part of her—all of her varied personalities—would find integration in Christ by this sacred moment of immersion. Then I baptized her, plunging her deep in the water where every part of her, including all those personalities, was surrounded and enveloped in water. She dried off. We prayed over her again, and she disappeared.

Until at least five years later. As mysteriously as she had vanished, she returned to our church and asked to speak privately with my wife and me. In graphic detail she told us about all the trauma she had faced that caused each of the various personalities. We sat there and listened. The hardest part of those few hours was not listening to the litany of pain one person had endured. The hardest part was to not sit there gape-mouthed in awe that she is alive after all she suffered. She wanted to tell us all of the various traumatic experiences, because after the baptism she had experienced five years earlier, not one of the multiple personalities had presented themselves ever again. It was such an amazing occurrence that her doctor brought in a specialist to determine what had happened. After a conclusive study, his only determination was that the miraculous occurred. My wife and I were stunned. She asked that we pass this story on to whoever would be willing to listen. We promised we would, and she left us to go on her way as a fully integrated soul through water baptism.

Water has always played an important role in spirituality. Water was a witness to creation in the beginning of time. You may remember that Genesis 1:2 informs us that the Spirit hovered over the deep. That word *hover* in Hebrew is the same word used for a bird covering its young with its wings. So this moment is pictured as the waters of the deep bubbling in anticipation of creation as the Spirit of God compassionately embraced it. Water was a witness to creation. Water was a witness as the children of Israel journeyed through the Red Sea's cavernous depths to escape the pursuing Egyptian army. Water stood as a witness when Jesus began his earthly ministry by being immersed by John the Baptist. So many major events of creation and re-creation were witnessed by water.

Water also stood witness throughout Palestine when the Levitical priests prepared themselves for Temple service. Before these priests entered the Temple to serve in any capacity, they would first be immersed in a mikvah. The mikvah was a fresh water pool used for ceremonial cleansing. The priest would walk down the steps of the mikvah, be immersed in water, and then would be ushered into Temple service.

The same mikvah was used when a person who was not born ethnically a Jew wished to commit to the Jewish faith. These adherents known as proselyte Jews would tread the steps of the mikvah and be immersed in water. Upon exiting the mikvah, the newly formed believer was wrapped in a white robe and would hear the words, "Now you are under the wing of the *Shekinah*." Once again, just as in creation, the Spirit of God, the *Shekinah*, the embodiment of the moral excellence of God himself, is embracing new creation.

Once we discover these Jewish images of immersion, it becomes clear that baptism is not just a one-time event but a means by which we live our lives. Water spiritually serves as a witness to life and to new ways of living. Whether it is the cosmos, the children of Israel, or Levitical priests or proselytes, water is the matrix that leads to new ways of living. Water is a transitional component for embracing new status and new identity. With this in mind, the question then becomes: what if I lived daily from a place of baptism? What if that moment of cleansing and commitment became the platform by which I lived my life, made decisions, and determined behavior? This is the proposition that shapes the next faith lesson—immersion—which states:

> *Your growth is commensurate with*
> *your depth of exposure.*

As Christians, if we are to grow in faith and spirit, it is necessary that we immerse ourselves in the culture of Christ. To help us understand this, let's define culture. Culture is the behaviors, beliefs, and characteristics of a particular social, ethnic, or age group. Culture is the sum total of a particular group's laws, stories, foods, experiences, songs, rituals, and practices. All things done as an initiate of that culture are shaped by these elements of the culture. Everything is captured under the umbrella of that culture.

I love subcultures. I never cease to be amazed by the color and life of various subcultures. They have their own language and their own ways of seeing the world through the filter of their subculture. Golfers belong to a subculture. They share some of the same experiences and frustrations. Bikers, with their massive motorcycles, are part of a subculture. There is lore involved and places where they congregate. Even addicts that share the same vice are part of a subculture.

I remember being invited into the subculture of heroin addicts as I built bonds with an amazing woodworker named Brad. Brad has an infectious personality. To know him is to be drawn into his laughter and the sincerity in his eyes. But Brad will admit that he is good at two things. He is a great woodworker, and he is good at scoring heroin. Around ten o'clock one night, I received a call from Brad. He was holed up in a local hotel room on a binge. He was crying out for help. "Eric, you will get here, or the dope man will. Whoever gets here first is the one I leave with, and I've already called my dealer." I had to play catch up, and his supplier had a headstart. It helped that I was only ten minutes away from his hotel. I won the race. The prize was to take Brad to get some coffee and talk about life. He told me about his subculture. He told me about the hunger for heroin, the ups and downs of a heroin high. He told me about acts of justice and compassion in crack dens and alleys. He shared with me how he begins each day with a plan to raise or steal money, where to buy, where and how to shoot up. This discussion smacked of the calm and calculated tone of a golfer talking about how he perfected his swing or a long distance runner talking about the emotional and physical terrain of a marathon. Heroin was a subculture to Brad. It had its shared ethics, laws, habits, and stories. There was a codified language and process that is similar to the way an artist functions within her aesthetic.

Keep in mind, I am doggedly committed to identifying all these activities, whether it is golf, art, or even addiction, as subculture. All of these activities or ways of living are always in a subservient role to a larger culture. There is a culture or meta-reality that all other strata of society function under, whether it is acknowledged or not. This culture is the Christ-culture or, as Scripture calls it, the Kingdom of God.

What becomes dangerous for us all is the moment that Christ and his Kingdom-reality are relegated to one aspect of a specific subculture versus being what I would call prime-culture. When Christ becomes just one aspect of one's subculture, Jesus becomes the white person's Christ or the black person's Christ or the liberal's Christ, the fundamentalist's or the evangelical's Christ, etc. The teachings of Christ merely serve as a specific subculture's predetermined ideology. The only aspects that are highlighted become the ones that serve that subculture. Then the only way the other (whoever that other might be) can find entry into said subculture is to divest themselves of certain aspects of who they are in order to be admitted into the subculture's relationship with Christ. That subculture often reserves their affections and access to the things of Christ until the other subscribes to the varied aspects of the subculture they are attempting to connect with. Why is Sunday the most segregated day of the week? The answer is because the *Logos*, the very causal and sustaining agent of the entire cosmos, has been reduced to but a part of a certain group's culture instead of being affirmed as prime culture itself.

The Christ-culture

All of us must come to understand that in Christ there is no other culture. In Christ, everything becomes subculture. "For we were all baptized by one Spirit into one body—whether Jews or Greeks, slave or free—and we were all given the one Spirit to drink" (1 Cor. 12:13). And Paul informs us in Colossians 3:11 that "here there is no Greek or Jew, circumcised or uncircumcised, barbarian, Scythian, slave or free, but Christ is all, and is in all."

Part of the larger redemptive plan of God is that everyone finds their way under the umbrella of the culture of Christ. For this to occur, those currently in Christ must immerse themselves in the Christ-culture. This is why discipleship becomes such an integral part of God's redemptive plan. Discipleship is a part of the immersion experience.

Imagine the moment: you are part of the beleaguered ragtag bunch of followers of the Messiah known as the Twelve. One of you turned in your leader to the authorities, which led to his grue-some torture and execution. One of your group turned on your leader. He disowned all that you all have been working on for the last three years and denied even being a part of him and you. Then word has spread that, after being dead and buried for three days, your Master has risen again and has been seen by several trustworthy sources. Out of fear you now find yourselves hunkered down together behind locked doors. As you wrestle with the weight of these incredible events, and perhaps with your own cowardice, there he is: Jesus. The risen Messiah is standing right there before you. Having disregarded locked doors, denial, and cowardice itself, Jesus is standing in your midst, and he says to you and your awed companions, "Go make disciples of all men." You see, Jesus is functioning on an assumption about how people think and learn. That assumption is that people grow when they are surrounded by experiences that contain the values and meanings to be learned.

We see Jesus functioning on that same assumption during his earthly ministry. He says to the Twelve, for example, "Let us go to the wedding. Help me pass out the multiplied loaves and fish. Attend the teaching sessions on the sides of mountains and on the seaside with me. Eat meals with me. Let us sleep in the same places and travel the same roads, because these experiences will transfer what needs to be learned. Being saturated in those things that contain the values and meanings of the Christ-culture will transfer those values and meanings into your hearts and lives." This is why the initial participants in the Christ-culture were called "the Way" (Acts 9:2). Following Christ was a way of life—not just one aspect of one's own way of life.

The dynamic of immersion as it relates to your faith functions much like the physics behind the keel of a boat. The ship's keel became necessary when ships got larger and sailed longer distances. The keel brings stability to a sailing vessel. The deeper the keel, the greater the stability. So it is that the deeper we are immersed in the culture of Christ, the greater our spiritual stability and growth in faith.

Each of us needs to ask: how immersed am I in the culture of Christ? To clarify that question, I want to highlight this subtle but extraordinarily interesting moment in Mark 3, a moment that brings into stark relief what it means to be immersed in the Christ-culture.

> There came then his brethren and his mother, and,
> standing without, sent unto him, calling him. And
> the multitude sat about him, and they said unto him,
> Behold, thy mother and thy brethren without seek for
> thee. And he answered them, saying, Who is my mother,
> or my brethren? And he looked round about on them
> which sat about him, and said, Behold my mother and
> my brethren! (31–34 KJV)

What do you think the crowd expects to happen here? They expect Jesus to stop what he is doing in order to be drawn into the concerns of his earthly mother and brothers. This is what familial ties demand. We gravitate to the issues and concerns at the center of a familial issue or concern. Instead of moving or shifting his focus, though, Jesus asks a question and makes a remarkable gesture. It is a gesture that highlights so much of the ethos and tenor of the Jesus project and the Christ-culture. And Jesus explains his actions by saying to the surprised crowd, "Whosoever shall do the will of God, the same is my brother, and my sister, and mother" (Mark 3:35 KJV).

"Who really makes up the members of my family?" Jesus asks. And he answers his own question by the gesture he makes. Scripture says Jesus looked round at those that sat "about" him. That word translated *about* in the King James Version not only can refer to location but also to purpose. The word in Greek is *peri*, which means not only "about" but also "on account of." These people who are "about" Jesus positionally are also "about" Jesus dispositionally. They are there on account of him. They are tuned in, saturated, and immersed in the things of Christ, and this becomes the basis for familial connection.

Immersion precedes significant growth in whatever we do. When we sink deep in a culture of spiritual growth, our faith begins to flourish. The move toward greater faith is a move toward immersion into a culture of growth, love, and encouragement.

Culture of Growth

We find another truly remarkable moment in the life of Christ in the Gospel of Mark. After Jesus teaches an ever-growing multitude of people, he turns to his closest followers, the twelve apostles, and says to them, "Let us cross over to the other side." What a provocative statement! It's a statement filled with uncertainty and mystery. It is a statement so riddled with voids that I can't help but imagine that the apostles' first thought had to be: Oh, no!

Crossing to the other side means moving into unsafe territory. It means moving out of a Jewish context and moving into a Gentile context where there is a reasonable chance of becoming ceremonially unclean. Sure enough, when they do cross to the other side of the lake, they find themselves in a place filled with pigs and dead men's bones. Scripture paints this amazingly vivid picture where as soon as Jesus and his apostles make landfall and step out of the boat, a man with an unclean spirit comes up to them, a fellow who has the unmitigated gall to live in the community graveyard. Scripture says he is surrounded by death and dying and the filth of things unclean. Not only this, but internally he is filled with a legion of unclean spirits. To say the least, this poor man is unable to escape the images of death and decay—unable, that is, until Jesus comes and frees him from an environment steeped in thoughts of death. Jesus speaks words of release, and the unclean spirits leave the man and enter a nearby herd of swine. Driven by the spirits, the swine run violently down the slope of the mountain and into the water, where they drown. When people from the surrounding towns and villages come to see what all of the commotion is about, they see the man "who had been possessed by the legion of demons, sitting there, dressed and in his right mind" (Mark 5:15).

I bring up this fascinating occurrence in Jesus's life because, soon afterward, the man who was once demon-possessed begs Jesus to let him go with him. Jesus says no, but commands this transformed man to go home. "Don't stay where you are!" Jesus instructs him. Go home and tell everyone about your transformation and how it occurred. The man did Jesus one better. He didn't just go home. He went to the ten villages surrounding his home to let everyone know that change, transformation, and growth can really occur through a fresh encounter with Jesus.

Previously that man's environment made it conducive for death to reign in his life. Everything around him, whether it was the dead men's bones or the graves or the smell and stench of pigs, made it conducive for stagnation to persist.

How many times are our lives the same way? We desire growth and development but surround ourselves with things that discourage growth and development. It is incumbent upon us all to immerse ourselves in a culture of growth and development. Everywhere we look we need to see examples of real, substantive transformation and growth. Let's immerse ourselves in the teachings of Jesus and in the lives of people in the Bible who accepted the challenge of growth and development. The biographies of past saints who overcame the obstacles and roadblocks to faith should be staple reading. All around us should be constant reminders that stagnation is no longer a reasonable option in light of God's gracious gift of love.

Love

As a minister of a church, I find one of the great joys is learning as I teach. I once felt like my responsibility during a Bible class was to impart information to those in need of greater clarity on a theological concern or on some special jog or turn Christ made during his life. Gradually, though, I began to figure out that our time together as we study the Bible is an exercise of three-way exchange. In that sacred time and space of communion, God is thick in the room, I am there as a mere facilitator in this great exchange, and also present are my class, people with varied experience and insight. Class time is a rich experience of exchange.

I found this truly to be the case when June started attending one of my classes. For decades June lived her life modestly as the wife of a boisterous and lovable veterinarian. He had story upon story about delivering calves and tending to horses. His personality was so big it filled the room. June sat quietly in the small corner his personality left room for. She held vigil over the highs of his jovial outbursts and stood as witness to the crashes his personality inevitably would create. All of that corner-sitting and watch-keeping June did for so long shaped her somehow. It molded her character and gave her a rich repose that only a life attached to the life of the party could create. Every time I'd bring up a topic during a class, she would raise her hand and add, "Yes, Eric, you know what you are saying is true, but none of it makes any difference if there is not love." It didn't matter what the topic was, or the depth of the concept posed. June's natural inclination was to consistently remind me, much like a metronome reminds the musician of the time signature, that love is at the root of all that is of God. This was her continued comment, her insistent plea. The first and second time she did that in a class, I was taken aback, maybe due to the frankness with which June said it. Or maybe I was taken aback by the embarrassment of forgetting to mention love. Soon I came to expect this comment from June. Then I began to delight in the regularity of her statement. While it took longer than I would like to admit, I began to learn from June. She had learned something from all of those years of observation and making room for her husband's larger-than-life presence. It was something I needed to learn—to never ever forget that love is the very fiber of God's plan. Love is the thread that weaves the story and holds the redemptive narrative together.

Love is the bond that held God the Father, God the Son, and God the Spirit together before there was time. Love is the reason that this God who exists in the oneness of community conceived of creating humanity. Love is the reason for his covenant to be made and kept.

It's powerful to immerse ourselves in the kind of love June talked about. Here, we are not talking about romantic love or media-outlet love. Here, we are talking about the love that is found in tears, blood, and commitment. This is the kind of love that thrives on inconvenience.

I think it is wonderful that Jesus calls himself the bread of life. Jesus is truly that. Before the time of being concerned with carbs and living gluten-free, bread was the staple of life. For most people, bread meant life. If there was bread to be had, there was hope for sustaining life till the next day. As a matter of fact, Jesus, the bread of life, was born in Bethlehem, a town name that means the house of bread. God provided bread for the children of Israel in the desert for forty years of wandering. Bread came from heaven, they would say, as they would gather up manna after the dew burned off at the start of their day. Jesus multiplied loaves of bread. Jesus broke bread and offered it to his followers as an example of who he was and the role he had in their lives. Jesus was and is bread.

I love this because the very nature of bread embodies love. I started learning how to bake bread several years ago. I used it as a stress reliever and even as a spiritual discipline. With the hectic nature of my role as a minister, I needed something to slow me down, something where I could use my hands. I would do contemplative bread baking . . . if you can believe something like that can be done. I mindfully took the flour and measured precisely. I carefully tended to the yeast and nurtured it with sugar and warm water. I coaxed the dough into rising as the fermentation process began. I tried to get a sense of the dough's surroundings, monitoring the temperature in the room as it was rising.

I made some pretty big mistakes when I started this bread-making process. I must have killed at least seventeen packets of yeast when I started. Yeast is a living, functioning element in the bread-making process, and either my water was too hot for the yeast I put in or I would wait too long to put the yeast in my bread. Whatever the motive or weapon used, I was a yeast-murderer for several months. Other yeast packages screamed when they saw me coming down the aisle at the grocery store. I could hear the fear inside each packet of yeast as it trembled when I picked it up. It was bad.

One time my wife's family joined us for lunch, and I decided to make fresh bread for our sandwiches. I made two loaves of the most beautiful white bread you'd ever want to see. The house smelled of fresh-baked bread as they entered our home. Anticipation of a delicious lunch rose as I, with great deliberateness, cut slices of the bread. We piled the slices high with deli meats and garnishments. I beamed with pride until we all took the first bite. It was the blandest bread we'd ever tasted. In my haste I had forgotten to put salt in the bread. It looked good, but it was awful. My wife thought the loaves were so beautiful that she took the remaining loaf, shellacked it, and used it as a decorative center piece for our dining room table. That loaf mocked me every time we ate at that table. It mocked me, and I could hear it whisper every time we sat at the table, "Love does not function in haste because love thrives on tending to the details. Like salt, Eric! Really, did you forget the salt?"

Jesus is the bread of life because love can be found in the very nature of bread. Bread is about love. Love is the grinding of grain, kneading of dough, feeding and proofing the yeast, and waiting. While all of these things are inconvenient and could certainly be bypassed by using a breadmaker or just running to the store and buying a loaf, bread baking takes the attentiveness of a lover. The bread rebels or has an aftertaste of bitterness if the baker doesn't love as he bakes.

The same is true when we love one another. Nothing is convenient about love. Love never works on our schedule. Love always demands more time than we have allotted. Love requires more patience than we measured out, requires more of us than we intended to give, and costs more than we planned to spend.

When we dare to immerse ourselves in that kind of love, we are immersed into the culture of Christ. Christ always gave more, spent more time, and offered more of himself than any earthly man would dare to sacrifice. It's there in the grinding, kneading, and baking process of love that we meet God in his full splendor. It's in the fiery furnace where the three defiant men encounter Deity.

June was so right. It doesn't matter if we are pondering eschatology or remnant theology. If we are not talking about those things in the context of love, we are not talking about anything related to God. I often thought in those classes where June reminded us all to love that our omnipresent God was standing and cheering his daughter's insistence that love be talked about more than any other topic.

Encouragement

Encouragement is such a key component in the Christ-culture. I believe this is because discouragement is such a big part of Satan's strategy to derail the Jesus project.

Satan plays on our fears or in this case our *dis*couragement. If the devil can stir up our fears, he can do two things simultaneously—stop us in our tracks and chip away at our trust in God. Either one of those outcomes alone derails our participation in the Kingdom, but both of them certainly jettison our participation.

Spiritual Disciplines

A spiritual discipline is a scripturally sound, time-tested means of placing ourselves in the trajectory of God's will for our spiritual growth and development.

Typically the list of spiritual disciplines includes activities such as worship, study, prayer, silence, solitude, fasting, service, celebrating, and generosity. They often are broken down into the two different classifications of taking-in disciplines and taking-away disciplines. The taking-in disciplines are worship, study, and prayer. Subsequently, the taking-away disciplines are fasting, silence, solitude, and generosity. I also have a list of disciplines that I call creative disciplines. I employ them for specific issues I encounter.

Maybe it is my upbringing or just my personality, but I have always had an issue with authority. Many people of my generation bristle at the thought of authority, even while we see the necessity for it. Regardless of what causes the bristling, I know I need to place myself under the authority of God. If I am going to continue to call him Lord, I must be willing to live under his Lordship as best I can. Even though I cannot see God clearly, I want to be able to live up to my declaration that he is Lord of my life. So I began to ask, "What discipline can I employ to train myself to live under authority?"

If I could honor his authority in a small thing, I concluded, perhaps it would lead to my honoring his authority in even greater things. My plan was to drive the speed limit at all times, regardless of whether I was late or not and whether everyone else was driving the speed limit or not. I was going to drive under the authority of those little black-and-white signs. Signs that seemed to be popping up everywhere now that I decided to drive the speed limit. Suddenly they were everywhere. The limits of the speeds they wanted me to drive seemed so much slower than I usually drove, because they were. I discovered that I was speeding everywhere I went. In the small college town where I ministered to a church, I found the speed limit on most of the streets I needed to drive on was a mere thirty-five miles per hour. It was so hard to do. It broke me down constantly. Especially since I had moved from driving in Los Angeles to driving in this small town. Before I started this discipline, I drove in this small town like I was on the 405 Freeway in Los Angeles (which, if you haven't been there, is notorious for bad driving). I cut people off left and right and never understood why people were honking at me and making lewd gestures with their fingers or, more to the point, a specific finger. That's how we drive in L.A. We cut each other off and drive fast and whip around in large cars as if we were driving tiny bumper cars.

Once I began employing this creative discipline of driving the speed limit, I expected the honking and finger gesturing to end. To the contrary, it continued and may even have got worse once I started driving under authority. While driving like a wild man was bad, what was worse was driving like a sane one. While my fast and furious way of driving upset people, this new restrained way of driving convicted them. This driving under authority called into question their ability to drive within the bounds authority demanded. As I slumped in resignation behind the wheel while others passed me honking, I came to a new realization. It occurred to me that if we have a problem with following these street signs that are ubiquitously present for all to see, how hard is it to follow a God we cannot see.

I can't say that I continuously follow the speed limit set by those signs any more than I can say that I always follow God as obediently as I should. But I can say that, because of that discipline, my soul now knows with a greater degree of clarity when I'm being disobedient.

It's important to say again as we discuss spiritual disciplines that we are merely placing ourselves in the trajectory of a growth process God ultimately controls, and you understand trajectory. We employ it all of the time. It's how I met my wife.

We met in college, and from the first meeting I knew I was not in her league. There was not a chance I could date someone as classy and refined as she was. At that time, I was a leather-jacketed, cowboy-hat-wearing bouncer at a bar. She was stunning, refined, and composed. At that time, a good time for me was a basketball game, a six-pack of beer, and a bag of chips. She seemed to float on rainbows as she dined on petit fours and drank herbal tea. I mean completely out of my league. But something was so compelling about her that I had to make at least some kind of contact. My plan was to stand in places where I might "just happen to run into her." We had a student commons that held the food court as well as the bookstore. This commons area also had the TV tuned to the soap opera everyone happened to be into at the time. I knew if she was not going to class, she would either be heading through the commons to grab lunch, catch a few scenes of her favorite soap, or walk through as a shortcut to wherever she was headed. So there I stood, uncomfortably cool, waiting for her to arrive. I was placing myself in her trajectory in the hopes of some sort of relational encounter.

The same is true for spiritual disciplines. We place ourselves in a particular orientation, hoping for some relational encounter. As we explore the disciplines, this is critically important for us to understand for two reasons. First, growth does not occur by our own tenacity and determination, but through relational encounter. Spiritual disciplines are much like any other type of discipline, except for these characteristics. Much like working out, learning to play an instrument, or taking martial-arts classes, spiritual disciplines function through repetitive action carried out for an extended period of time. Through these repetitive actions you train your body to function a certain way to execute an intended aim.

Spiritual disciplines, at first glance, seem exactly like any other type of discipline. This is true until we get to the relational-encounter component.

What makes spiritual disciplines different from any other discipline is the fact that most other disciplines are incumbent upon one's own tenacity and fortitude to achieve a particular aim, whether our goal is greater upper body strength, the ability to play complex rhythms on a drum set, or running long distances. Spiritual disciplines rely not on one's own strength but on the work of the Spirit of God. It is God, and specifically God's Spirit, who works to achieve our spiritual growth and development. This is seen in Galatians 5:22 where the aims of love, joy, peace, patience, kindness, goodness, faithfulness, gentleness, and self-control are not described as fruit we must bear, but as fruits of the Spirit that the Spirit is committed to bear in our lives. The disciplines of prayer, worship, silence, solitude, and fasting place us in the trajectory where we encounter God in a great depth of relationship, and it is in his presence that we are given those gifts of refined character. That character equips us to love God, ourselves, and our neighbors with a wholehearted love, which is the ultimate end of all spiritual disciplines. To achieve the depth of character we receive with these disciplines but not to use them to love is a waste of time and of energy of the Holy Spirit.

It's a waste I understand full well. While living in Los Angeles, I had the pleasure of working out with a lot of people in the television and film industry. We would spend two hours a day working out, lifting weights, and drinking energy smoothies, and then we'd work out some more. I was terrible at it. I mostly liked the smoothies. I worked out with some guys that really knew what they were doing. Muscles popped out all over these guys. They celebrated a new cut or bulge of muscle on their arms or abs. And they were ripped! When I would invite these guys over to our house to hang out, some chore would need to get done—something like lifting a box, moving something around, building or repairing something. These guys with all of those muscles would be ineffective for the task because they only knew how to use the mass of muscle they had to lift weights and nothing else. They did not know how to apply their strength to anything except to gain more muscle. The same is true when we seem to grow spiritually but cannot apply this growth to acts of love and compassion. It becomes a huge waste.

Essential Narrative

We are the stories we tell, recall, and remember. I come from a storytelling family. When I was too young to be listening, I remember sneaking into the hallway of our home when my uncles and aunts convened in our living room. The smell of cigarette smoke and laugher hung thick in the air. It was the seventies, and the purple shag carpet held vigil with the orange, paisley, swivel occasional chair as bards, soothsayers, and griots told family stories in tones so loud it shook the doorframe I leaned against. Some of those stories I knew were true. Others I wished they weren't. They were their stories. They were our stories. Those stories made us who we were as a family, and I loved them. While I spent the better part of a decade as a commissioned playwright, my older brother was the better storyteller. He is still a storyteller. Always was. He made up stories of superheroes for me off the top of his head. Now he holds court in that same living room, telling stories about his daughters or his clients and stories of our uncles and aunts telling their stories. We are the stories we tell.

Earlier I mentioned Joshua's re-covenanting with God and the children of Israel in Shechem and his telling of the essential narrative. This wasn't the last time this was done in the Bible. All through Scripture we see people at critical points breaking out in the essential narrative. Peter does this. Stephen does this before he is stoned. Paul continues the tradition of rehearsing the story of a good God and a fallen world. They tell the story of patriarchs and prophets. They share the story of Moses and the mighty hand of God that brought freedom to the oppressed. Over and over in the Bible this story is retold and gains momentum every time it is spoken. The sweep of history is in this essential narrative. The story of Jesus Christ is subsumed into this traditional narrative and becomes the very reason this narrative even began. This is why it is the essential narrative, because without this collection of proclaimed events we cease to have any significance. If these events never occurred, there is no longer a reason for reason. There is no life for the living. We are the stories we tell, recall, and remember.

We have to immerse ourselves in this essential narrative. We must find in these events our dwelling place. These retold events are our haven and our home. In this narrative, we find our identity and our trajectory. This essential narrative is the deep water in which we are immersed.

This calls for a serious commitment to reading the word of God, and not reading just for the sake of reading, even if there is much that can be derived from that. I am talking about the type of reading where you don't get through the text but the text gets through to you. This is where *Lectio Divina*, divine reading, is encouraged. We ponder, meditate, and chew on each word and phrase of Scripture so that God can speak through his word. We absolutely need to understand the meaning and context of Scripture, but that is merely the shore of the essential narrative. The call is to come out into the deep where immersion takes place. This type of reading requires living in the text and seeing who you are in the text. Are you the one asking Jesus for water to be turned into wine? Are you the grateful steward who has more wine to give when there was nothing else to offer? Or are you the water that has been turned into something greater than what was once intended? Immersion into Scripture requires familiarity with the shore but also the courage to allow the Bible to speak from a place of great depth.

When we immerse ourselves in the culture of Christ, a culture of growth, love, spiritual disciplines, and the essential narrative, we find ourselves soaked. These cultural elements fill every fissure and crevice of our being. The things of Christ find their way into every aspect of our lives. None of our hidden places are spared from this immersion. This is why immersion is so important, because this act touches all that we are and thereby becomes all that we are.

It is Christ's intent to immerse us in experiences and images to define who we are, in order to address those things that we aren't. We are not our obsessive thoughts. We are not the sum total of the mistakes of our past. We are not the torrent of our emotions which often set us adrift. Immersion into the Christ-culture redefines us as well as defines what must be jettisoned in our lives.

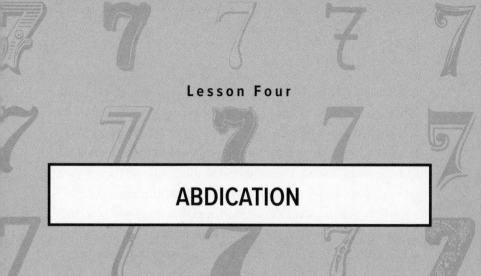

ABDICATION

*Your level of growth is commensurate
with your level of sacrifice.*

'D LIKE TO SHARE WITH YOU A BIT OF THE REAL-LIFE STORY OF Charles Gonsoulin of Los Angeles, because he is a man who could speak to us intimately about the topic we're discussing.

In 2005, Charles fell head over heels in love with a young lady who lived in Quebec, Canada. With Charles in Los Angeles and with her in Quebec, the distance dogged him. Charles could not legally enter Canada due to a twenty-year-old crime committed in his youth, and due to financial constraints, she could not afford to visit him. So in February of that year, Gonsoulin took a bus to North Dakota and decided to walk the sixteen-hundred miles to get to the one he loved. During his long hike, temperatures dipped below minus-fifteen degrees. On February 23, Charles was found wandering on a golf course in the middle of a storm, delirious from hypothermia. Suffering from severe frostbite, he was rushed to the hospital. They had to amputate all of his fingers and toes. As he contemplated the loss of so much, his comment to the reporter was, "It is better to have loved and to have lost than never to have loved at all. It was all worth it for me. It's the difference between sitting around dreaming about things and going out and getting them."

My response to Charles's behavior and statement?

Why would anybody be that stupid?! What is he . . . crazy?!

Despite the fact that I think this guy was insane, he brings to life a profound truth: Love demands sacrifice.

The fourth lesson of faith is abdication:

> *Your level of growth is commensurate*
> *with your level of sacrifice.*

Three Biblical Approaches to Spiritual Growth

One of the things we have to keep in the forefront of our minds is that there is not just one way for faith to grow. Paths to growth are as varied as those on the path itself. We often limit ourselves and others by the perception that there is only one way to grow in Christ. Everyone's growth is going to look a bit different from everyone else's. While the means to growth varies, I think it is important to highlight three paths in particular as we look at abdication.

Three significant trajectories of growth are displayed in Scripture. We often encounter a progressive moving toward, an interior acceptance of a new reality, as well as a return or renewal of what once was.

- There is a movement forward.
- There is a localized embrace.
- And there is a return to the past.

Moving Forward

Ephesians 4 says,

> Then we will no longer be infants, tossed back and forth
> by the waves, and blown here and there by every wind
> of teaching and by the cunning and craftiness of men in
> their deceitful scheming. Instead, speaking the truth in
> love, we will in all things grow up into him who is the
> Head, that is, Christ. (14–15)

Here we are talking about forward progression.

Inward Acceptance

The Bible also talks of growth as inward movement toward acceptance of some new reality.

Any time the apostle Paul calls the church saints, or beloved of God, or new men and women, he is asking us to consider a move towards accepting some new conferred reality. He is asking us to claim some new status that has already been given to us. This is so masterful of Paul. Whether we are looking at the growth of a faith community, the expansion and development of a business, or even the maturing of our children, we have to acknowledge the impact of positive or negative naming. When Paul gives the church the name of saints, he does not for a moment believe that they have attained the level of perfection associated with sanctification. If that was the case, most of his letters to churches would be very brief. After he calls them saints, he begins reproving them for faults and failures they need to correct. Paul's idea is that people and institutions rise to the expectations set for them. If we name ourselves as failures, we immediately move toward that established negative expectation. If we tell our children they will amount to nothing, our prediction has a really good chance of coming true. It is in our nature to live into the names and expectations given.

While serving at a church, I made a point of affirming the church leadership whenever I could. Whether it was in public or in committee meetings or with individual time spent with each one of them, I made a point of offering affirmation and setting the expectation that we were more than what we or others thought. We were more than we even believed. It made such a difference in the life of that church. In some small way, we took on the nature of our Father, who "calleth those things which are not, as though they were" (Rom. 4:17 KJV). Notice these scriptures: "For both He who sanctifies and those who are sanctified are all from one Father; for which reason He is not ashamed to call them brethren" (Heb. 2:11 NASB). We have been sanctified. God confers to us a status of holiness. At the point that we give ourselves over to this relationship in Christ, God places us in his heart where he holds all things holy. This amazing blessing of sanctification does not end there. Due to this connection with Christ, God sets us aside for divine use. The gift of sanctification offers with it a promise of purpose. We are not meant for aimlessness. All of us are here for a divine reason. We can give ourselves fully over to an enterprise with eternal implications. Our responsibility, if we so choose, is to move to an inner acceptance of this reality.

In his word, God places before us so many other realities that we must accept as reality. We are his children. We are beloved. We are the recipients of revelation and enlightenment. We are given a new way of living and a new way of seeing how life functions. All of these truths become significant in our lives only when we accept them as reality.

A Return or Renewal of What Once Was

The Bible also talks of our returning to or reclaiming aspects we once lost, in order for growth to occur. Throughout Scripture, restoration or renewal are discussed. Romans 12:2 commands us to renew our minds. We also have this incredible moment in the life of Jesus's followers when they are attempting to jockey for position and figure out who is the most prominent disciple. This is how Jesus chooses to weigh in on their conversation:

> And they were bringing children to Him so that He
> might touch them; but the disciples rebuked them. But
> when Jesus saw this, He was indignant and said to them,
> "Permit the children to come to Me; do not hinder them;
> for the kingdom of God belongs to such as these. Truly I
> say to you, whoever does not receive the kingdom of God
> like a child will not enter it at all." (Mark 10:13–15 NASB)

Jesus's demand is for us to return to the consciousness of children. There must be a return to the consciousness of the new mind. A childlike, new mind sees reality with the thrill of wonder as well as humility. Children, also, possess infinite faith and infinite reliance on others. Jesus is teaching his followers that there is an ardent need to return to a consciousness of the zygote.

At the moment of inception a zygote is made. That zygote is filled with embryonic stem cells. The reason so much research is going on in regards to the harvesting of stem cells is because these cells possess the infinite possibility of becoming whatever the body needs. These cells are given the designation of being pluripotent. This means each cell can become, at the very least, two hundred different kinds of cells the human body needs. These cells hold infinite possibilities if given guidance.

This is the type of spiritual return we need. We need to return to a consciousness of infinite possibilities. We must return to that time when we, if given the proper guidance, can become whatever is needed in the body. Here I'm referring to the Body of Christ. Imagine being that pliable and malleable. A return is needed.

In Eden, before the Fall of humanity, we were working in partnership with God as caretakers of the world. It was a consciousness of infinite connection and infinite commitment. We need to return to that way of thinking. What a way of thinking! What a state of mind! A renewal of fresh and innovative thinking. Could this be what Christ meant when he spoke of new birth? Infinite faith, infinite possibilities, infinite connection, infinite commitment—isn't it great? Isn't that a renovated mind, a re-born mind, a renewed mind? Isn't that the way we need to think? How do I deal with the heartache I face? With a renewed mind that sees this heartache with infinite faith, infinite possibilities, infinite connection, infinite commitment? How do I deal with this brokenness I feel? With a renewed mind that sees this brokenness with infinite faith, infinite possibilities, infinite connection, infinite commitment. How do I deal with this challenge I must face as an individual or that we must face as a church or as a world? With a renewed mind that sees this challenge with infinite faith, infinite possibilities, infinite connection, infinite commitment. Not conformed to the world's thinking (the world's thinking is warped; it's skewed; it's repulsive). Not conformed to the world's thinking, but to a renewed, restored thinking predicated on relationship with God and responsiveness to his call—a renewed mind transformed by the righteousness of God.

For faith to grow and for our spirits to develop, there is often a need for a progressive moving toward, for an interior acceptance of a new reality, as well as for a return to or renewal of what once was. This is important for our discussion of abdication, because if movement is significant to growth, then we come to realize that whatever weighs us down hampers our growth. As Hebrews 12:1 says, "Since we are surrounded by such a great cloud of witnesses, let us throw off everything that hinders and the sin that so easily entangles."

Worthy of Sacrifice

There is an old story about two paddleboats. They left Memphis about the same time, traveling down the Mississippi River to New Orleans. As they traveled side by side, sailors from one vessel made a few remarks about the snail's pace of the other. Words were exchanged. Challenges were made, and the race began.

Competition became vicious as the two boats roared through the Deep South. One boat began falling behind. Not enough fuel. There had been plenty of coal for the trip but not enough for a race. As the boat dropped back, an enterprising young sailor took some of the ship's cargo and tossed it into the boilers. When the sailors saw that the supplies burned as well as the coal, they fueled their boat with whatever they could find. They won the race because they not only had more fuel to burn but, in so doing, lightened their load. Sacrifice was the key to the victory.

One question we have to ask: what is it about the nature of God that makes sacrifice so significant? Sacrifice is so difficult to do, hard to capture, and challenging to carry out consistently. It is incumbent upon us to find out why sacrifice is so significant to God. Maybe this discovery will motivate us to embrace it.

As we analyze the essence of the divine and how God functions, we find that at the heart of sacrifice are these two ideas. First, God sees everyone as being worthy of his sacrifice, and second, he is able to redeem whatever we lose for his sake and the sake of his gospel. This is what Jesus says to us as his followers:

> No one who has left home or brothers or sisters or
> mother or father or children or fields for me and the
> gospel will fail to receive a hundred times as much in
> this present age: homes, brothers, sisters, mothers, chil-
> dren and fields—along with persecutions—and in the
> age to come eternal life. (Mark 10:29–30)

God believes you are worth sacrificing for. You are so valued by God that he is willing to sacrifice to ensure greater and greater depths of intimacy. Whatever it takes, God is willing to do it if it means you will find your way into relationship with him. This is an absolutely life-changing thought. We can debate all day long about what gives a person value. The answers are as varied as the people who make the claims. We can't even discover how a person gains value until we come to the conclusion first that God deems us to be valuable.

Let's bask in the beauty of that notion first. Let's own this notion as the reality at the outset, because this has drastic implications for your life and the life of others. If God values you enough to die for you, you can believe that God feels this way about everyone else as well. God sees us all as worthy of sacrifice, which means we must see ourselves as well as others in that light. I want to see you as someone worth my giving my whole attention to. I must see you as someone worth giving my time to. God calls me to see everyone as someone to whom I am willing to sacrifice my right to be right. Ephesians 5:21 calls us to submit to one another out of reverence for Christ. Imagine a world where we all attempt to out-submit one another. As beautiful as that picture is, sacrifice and abdication are hard. At the core of who God is rests the notion that whatever we give up for one another, whether it is time, money, effort, energy, grace, mercy, or our rights, God is able to replace whatever is lost for and through his larger plan of redemption.

For growth there is a need for sacrifice or abdication. Abdication means to cast off or to relinquish. It also has the implication of renouncing a throne, high office, dignity, or function. What we are talking about here is not only ending something, but ending the influence and power associated with the relinquished function. Three areas of our lives must be addressed when we are talking about abdication: Sin, Self, and Substance. When we, under the power of the Holy Spirit of God, can make any headway in these three areas, we lighten our load and make greater speed toward our growth in so many areas of our life.

The Abdication of Sin

Everyone makes mistakes in life. We say the thing that shouldn't be said. We do the thing that shouldn't be done. In a moment of weakness, confusion, or brokenness, we behave in a way that is completely contrary to the will and way of God. When we think of abdication, we are not talking about the mistakes inherent in our up-and-down progression towards holiness. Here we are talking about a lifestyle of sin—when we find ourselves surrounded by, ruled over, and under the control of sin. Here we are talking about knowingly engaging in community-destroying behavior that is not a one-time occurrence but a consistent companion that compromises God's moral standard. We have to carry out the process of abdicating the abiding sin in our lives. This is the point of Romans 6:1–11:

> What shall we say, then? Shall we go on sinning so that grace may increase? By no means! We are those who have died to sin; how can we live in it any longer? Or don't you know that all of us who were baptized into Christ Jesus were baptized into his death? We were therefore buried with him through baptism into death in order that, just as Christ was raised from the dead through the glory of the Father, we too may live a new life. For if we have been united with him in a death like his, we will certainly also be united with him in a resurrection like his. For we know that our old self was crucified with him so that the body ruled by sin might be done away with, that we should no longer be slaves to sin—because anyone who has died has been set free

from sin. Now if we died with Christ, we believe that we
will also live with him. For we know that since Christ
was raised from the dead, he cannot die again; death no
longer has mastery over him. The death he died, he died
to sin once for all; but the life he lives, he lives to God.
In the same way, count yourselves dead to sin but alive
to God in Christ Jesus. (NIV 2011)

Paul states here emphatically that we can no longer abide in sin
because we have taken Christ's death as our own death. Is this too
hard a concept to fathom? Can you grasp the notion of owning
the consequences for someone else's death? It's certainly critical
to the Christ project. It's pivotal if I am to participate in the covenantal plan of unity, because if we merely die ourselves, we die and
along with us dies our influence. If my hatreds die or my drive to
manipulate dies, if my outbursts of rage, drunkenness, gossiping,
and indifference die, and yet I remain, the impact on the people
and the world around me becomes overwhelming.

Most young people who grow up in a Christian environment
tend to abandon their faith after two weeks in college. Because I
am historically a high achiever, I abandoned my faith about two
hours after my father dropped me off at the University of Missouri.
Sin was not a constant rain in my life. It was a crashing wave. The
decisions I made and the damage I inflicted on myself and others
in some way were legendary in that small college town. All the
while I knew I was doing wrong, and all the while I was trying to
understand this lifestyle in light of the truths I knew about Christ.
Eventually what I knew about Christ and the depth of intimacy we
had shared in my youth won out over that lifestyle of sin.

After many years of working and traveling, my wife and I found
ourselves back in this small college town after the birth of our first
son Canaan. I was working at the university as a student mentor

as well as an adjunct professor. Because so much of my life was centered on the university campus, my church invited me to serve as their campus minister. In a place that held the memories of so much evil and sin and violence and pain, I entered as a servant of God. As a matter of fact, one of the bars where I spent many nights immersed in sin had over the years become a coffee house. The new owners wanted to create a space where their son could have deep conversations of faith with his friends in a non-threatening environment. So this dive bar that was once aptly named Shattered was now a place where lives were being put back together. It became my primary office where I met with students and seekers to talk about faith in the context of life lived. It was one of the greatest gifts God has given to me. I had the ability to live as a redeemed person in a space where people used to know me as the hot mess that I once was.

It was almost like the man Jesus encounters on the shores of the Gennesaret in Mark 5. He has so many demons in his life that they are called Legion. He has such an army of voices, opinions, differing beliefs running through his person that it is as if he has a Roman legion of soldiers marching through his consciousness. But, after a fresh encounter with Christ, Scriptures say that those who once knew him as a wild man now see him "sitting, clothed and in his right mind." Imagine the influence this sight had on the people this man used to engage. The questions they asked must have piqued their interest in the Christ this man encountered.

I was that man. The opportunity God gave me in my old space was phenomenal.

This could only happen in light of the substitutionary status of Christ coming into play. The only way I could die yet live is because I took on Jesus's death. The only way Jesus's death could work in this way is if he is so inextricably connected to me and all of humanity that his death would be big enough to justify so great a substitution.

For his death to serve as a substitution for the spiritual death of the world, he had to be amazingly significant on a conscious level but also on a cosmic level. The person substituting his death for the death of all had to in some way be tied to the core fiber of reality. As we ponder this, the words of Colossians 1 come echoing from the distance:

> He is the image of the invisible God, the firstborn of all
> creation. For by Him all things were created, both in
> the heavens and on earth, visible and invisible, whether
> thrones or dominions or rulers or authorities—all
> things have been created through Him and for Him. He
> is before all things, and in Him all things hold together.
> He is also head of the body, the church; and He is the
> beginning, the firstborn from the dead, so that He
> Himself will come to have first place in everything. For
> it was the Father's good pleasure for all the fullness to
> dwell in Him, and through Him to reconcile all things
> to Himself, having made peace through the blood of His
> cross; through Him, I say, whether things on earth or
> things in heaven. (15–20 NASB)

The significance of Christ is big enough to warrant his death's making up for everyone else's. He is the cosmic Christ. He is the source and the means of creation itself. Jesus Christ is the *raison d'etre* for reality and reason itself. His being and purpose are so vast that his death has the magnitude to be sufficient to satisfy the weight of our collective spiritual death. Paul explains it like this in Romans 5,

> Consequently, just as the result of one trespass was
> condemnation for all men, so also the result of one act

of righteousness was justification that brings life for all men. For just as through the disobedience of the one man the many were made sinners, so also through the obedience of the one man the many will be made righteous.

The law was added so that the trespass might increase. But where sin increased, grace increased all the more, so that, just as sin reigned in death, so also grace might reign through righteousness to bring eternal life through Jesus Christ our Lord. (18–21)

The key to the process of abdication of sin is repentance. Repentance is an amazing multivalent word. But with all of the varied meanings of the word *repentance*, feeling bad and remorseful to the point of shame and guilt is not one of them. When pastors and preachers use the word *repentance* to cast shame and guilt on a suffering individual, they are playing into the hands of Satan. Not that there is not a place for guilt and even shame in spiritual growth and development, but when applied to repentance in an unhealthy way, shame and guilt are the tools of the devil. Specifically because they are used for manipulation and social control versus a real means of growth and development. Repentance is *metanoia*. It is transcendence to or a move toward a greater mind. That is its literal meaning—a turning toward a greater form or means of thinking. It is a turning from one form of allegiance to another. Keep in mind that allegiance functions from not only a place of consciousness, but from a place of consciousness that leads to specific behavior. Repentance is not mere mental ascent. It is mental ascent that motivates certain types of behavior. Repentance is the picture of you standing between two large mounds—one mound at your left and one at your right. If you can imagine that one of those mounds is a pile of your accumulated sins, all of them there, whether they are sins of jealousy, anger, addiction, sexual impurity—whatever those sins are. They are piled up all in one place before you. There is the pile with all of its ugliness and stench, and not only that, but also its power and influence. On the other side is the love of and promises of God stacked high in all of their majesty—all the love, all of the joys, all of the difficult commitments, right along with every promise of peace, rest, strength, and wisdom. There they are, with all of their splendor and glory, and not only that, but their power and influence as well. As you imagine these two mounds, questions come from above: What consciousness do you choose? Will you take a consciousness shaped by sickness, anxiety, scarcity, and division? Or will you turn toward an allegiance to a consciousness that is shaped by love, health, abundance, and unity? Both are hard. Each has consequences good and bad. But, repentance demands a choosing. It demands a resolute turning.

This resolute turning is pictured vividly in the book of Luke as Jesus moves closer and closer to his inevitable crucifixion and resurrection. Knowing that there would be the potential for external as well as internal pressure to avoid the inescapable nature of the cross, Jesus positioned himself in a way that led to accomplishing his goal. This positioning could not take place once the overwhelming challenge was upon him. That would have been far too late to begin his process, because of the enormity of the task before him. Jesus had to position himself far ahead of the challenge in order to better equip himself for the task at hand. In 9:51, Luke says that Jesus steadfastly set his face to go to Jerusalem. The word used in the original Bible language for "steadfastly set his face" is a compound word that places two different words together, both of them meaning to position one's self firmly. This resolute turning of repentance is a decision you make to plant yourself unwaveringly in a new way of thinking and being where sin is now thought of in completely different ways. This is true of self as well.

Abdication of Self

There has to be an abdication of sin, and there must be an abdication of self. The word *abdication* is critical as it relates to the renunciation of self, because abdication means not only to get rid of but also to voluntarily give up a throne. It means to move out of the way so that someone else can take the place of power.

The story of Robin Hood has been told over and over again. It somehow has captured the hearts and imaginations of people for generations, but we sometimes remember only the sword fights and green tights and miss the political intrigue of the story. The story is about Robin of Locksley, a young nobleman named an outlaw by Prince John because Robin shoots a deer on King Richard's land. Robin flees England and joins King Richard, known as Richard the Lion-Hearted, on the Crusade. Robin returns to England from fighting side by side with the king and hides from Prince John in Sherwood Forest, where he begins robbing the rich and giving to the poor. That is the main story, but we cannot miss the other story at play.

The other story is that of King Richard and his brother, Prince John. You see, while King Richard is away, his brother John is on Richard's throne. John is not king, but he is sitting where the King is supposed to sit. He occupies royal space, and John becomes used to that throne and does not want to leave it. He prefers that King Richard stay away or even die in battle. Whatever Richard does, John does not want him to come home, for that would force him to abdicate (get off of) his borrowed throne.

By this time in the story, John has become quite rich by taxing all of England. While the pretender to the throne, Prince John, is on the throne, the English people suffer. England stands with its head hung in shame, beaten down, drained dry, and humiliated, while bearing scars of coercion and being bullied into paying an unpayable debt. England suffers while John is on the throne. Prince

John, Guy of Gisburn, and the Sheriff of Nottingham are not so much worried about Robin Hood's stealing from the rich. What they are really worried about is Robin's political agenda, which is freeing up the throne so the good king can rule again in his rightful place. Robin's plan is to kick out John and all of his cronies so there is room on the throne for King Richard to return. Robin Hood's job is freeing up the throne so the rightful King can sit in his rightful place and carry out his rightful rule.

This story has captured our imaginations for generations because it is the story of our spiritual life. We often get quite comfortable sitting on thrones that belong to someone else. We believe we are the ones to make the decisive decisions for our lives, to determine how life is to go and what aspirations we should pursue. But what if we abdicate the throne of our hearts and free up enough space for the rightful king? Jesus is that King. He has risen from the dead to prove that he deserves to wear the crown. For real, substantive growth to occur, we need to daily abdicate our throne.

Consider Dallas Willard's definition of Kingdom as the range of a person's effective will. Everyone has kingdoms. If you run a business, to a certain degree it is a place where you can carry out your own will. If you are the head of your family, this is a place where you wield power. But say you don't have a business and you don't have a family that you oversee. Instead, you have a body. This becomes your kingdom because it is the place where you can carry out your effective will. Then Jesus Christ comes, and we commit ourselves to his lordship in all things. This sounds wonderful when we say it, but how does this become a reality and not just a pleasant platitude? We abdicate the thrones of our kingdoms to allow Jesus Christ to take his rightful place of power. Then the Kingdom of God becomes everywhere that God carries out his effective will.

This is why Jesus and his followers talked so much about dying to self:

Then said Jesus unto his disciples, If any man will come
after me, let him deny himself, and take up his cross,
and follow me. For whosoever will save his life shall lose
it: and whosoever will lose his life for my sake shall find
it. (Matt. 16:24–25 KJV)

Always bearing about in the body the dying of the Lord
Jesus, that the life also of Jesus might be made manifest
in our body. For we which live are always delivered unto
death for Jesus' sake, that the life also of Jesus might
be made manifest in our mortal flesh. So then death
worketh in us, but life in you. (2 Cor. 4:10–12 KJV)

I am crucified with Christ: nevertheless I live; yet not I,
but Christ liveth in me: and the life which I now live in
the flesh I live by the faith of the Son of God, who loved
me, and gave himself for me. (Gal. 2:20 KJV)

What does that look like? What does Christ living in me or ruling
my abdicated kingdom look like? There has been some fascinating psychological research coming out that speaks to this issue of
abdication of self.

Psychologist and author Mihaly Csikszentmihalyi has written a
series of books on creativity and a thing called "flow." His research
concerned what makes people happy. He specifically studied creative people, and he stumbled upon a profound biblical truth. As he
talked with people, he found they were the happiest when they were
working in a state of consumed focus, where everything seemed to
just click. Across the board, those interviewed described being in
a state of timeless, seemingly effortless, work. A state that they all
described as being in the flow of something. The research found
that people fell into this flow experience when their greatest preparation met their greatest challenge—when they were engaged in the

work they were ultimately meant to do, worked hard at perfecting that craft, and strove to do it at its highest level. When their highest level of skill met the highest degree of challenge, time slowed, and accomplishment became effortless, focus became clearer, and, what is most important to our discussion, those interviewed found a profound sense of loss of self. When engaged fully, the brain has an inability to be concerned about self.

A regimen of discerning God's will for your life, figuring out what he has determined you to be and do, not only doing it but training to do it better and better, and then engaging performance at a high level produces happiness and a healthy sense of loss of self.

Abdication of Substance

In the West, we live such blessed lives. I once heard someone suggest that we stumble over blessings here in America. We are so fortunate and live with such degrees of substance at our poorest that we are wealthier than 90 percent of the rest of the world. I have the fortune of having friends who have done quite well in their lives. They have reached a height of success most would envy. I am fortunate to get to be in relationship with them and to walk a life of faith with them so closely that I can see the advantages and profound disadvantages wealth can bring.

Once I had a dear friend roll up in a brand new, fire-red Lamborghini Testarosa. This is one of the fastest cars in the world, and it was not only beautiful but fresh from getting additional bells and whistles added. The factory tires were not enough. The factory paint job was not enough. The sound system it came with was nowhere near adequate for my friend. I mean this had to be one of the most expensive vehicles I've ever had the pleasure of standing near. I say "standing near" because, while given the opportunity to sit in it, I refused to for fear of breathing too hard on this magnificent automotive masterpiece. As I congratulated my friend on the purchase, he lamented, "But I really wanted the Bugatti." So, as I jiggled the keys to my car that desperately needed new brakes, an oil change, and the dent repaired, the thought came to mind, "WHAT?!"

Contentment is an elusive thing, especially if we have so much. The wanting always wants more. Want itself always wants newer, prettier, more powerful—just more of more. Discontent unsettles us. It keeps us off-center. Our lack of contentment serves to dismantle our relationships with God, with people, and with the deepest parts of who we are. Our deep-centered place, which functions in communion with God and serves as the healthiest place by which to live our lives, realizes that our contentment comes from God. This works really well until our disconnected selves, distracted by the world, attempt to satiate self with stuff and with the flawed notion that more always means better. The more we have, the more we realize that stuff does not satisfy, plenty can corrupt, and possessions have a tendency to weigh down our journey toward wholeness.

This is when the song penned by the great Johnny Mercer comes to mind and compels us to travel light. This is the joy that rests just beneath our attempts to simplify. See, this move toward simplicity serves to recalibrate our hearts to respond to what or, better yet, to who really brings true satisfaction. Simplicity, the discipline of divesting ourselves of our material possessions, reaffirms to us and God that he, and not our possessions, determines our identity. It is our abdication of substance.

The question we must ask is this: What motivates me to do this work? Why chose the path of abdication? The answer to these questions comes from the paradoxical teaching of Jesus Christ when he draws the attention of his followers to the transformative process of seed. Jesus hits them with the seemingly contradictory thought that in death there is life. "I tell you the truth," Jesus teaches, "unless a kernel of wheat falls to the ground and dies, it remains only a single seed. But if it dies, it produces many seeds. The man who loves his life will lose it, while the man who hates his life in this world will keep it for eternal life" (John 12:24–25). For the hard and seemingly unyielding seed to break forth and unleash what is within it, there must be a burial. If the seed is to reach its fullest potential and ultimately become what God intended it to be, there is a required abdication of life above ground and a required acceptance of this change and loss. Only then, in the incubator of darkness, dirt, and moisture, can hardened husks be loosened, roots be released, and the potential of fruitfulness be realized.

This is the motivator for abdication: only through dying do we truly live. What does Jesus teach us? *He that saves his life will lose it, but he that loses his life for my sake and for the gospel will save it.*

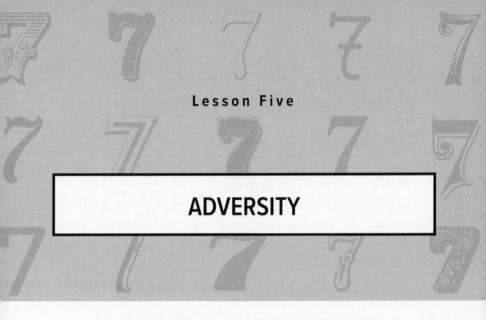

Lesson Five

ADVERSITY

*Your level of growth is commensurate with the
level of suffering you are willing to endure.*

THE TIME WAS 1999 IN PENNSYLVANIA, AND IT WAS A TIME OF choosing for Donald Wyman. He was by himself in the woods when he was pinned down by a falling tree. There was no way to get free. There was no one to help. With nothing but his pocket knife, he amputated his own leg, dragged himself to his pickup, and made it to the hospital. When they interviewed him, he said, "It was a terrible ordeal. I had a life-and-death situation, and that was my only choice—life or death. I have so much to live for that I did the only thing I could—I chose life."

There continually must be these moments of choosing daily—choosing between sin that enslaves us and God's love that frees us. In the midst of that choosing, there is adversity. The fearful moment of being pinned down. The agonizing moments of deciding. The cutting away. The pulling toward life. In these moments of choosing, growth can occur.

The fifth lesson of faith is adversity:

> *Your level of growth is commensurate with the*
> *level of suffering you are willing to endure.*

Exploration of Adversity

Journeying through the book of Job, we see a panoramic view of adversity and suffering. The reward for traveling through the twists and turns and dark alleys of that book is a powerful nugget of truth that changes everything. That truth is this: suffering and adversity have a necessary place in God's divine plan. Without adversity, there is no need to discover courage. Without hardship, our mettle is never tested. Without adversity, the bonds of camaraderie are not strengthened. Without hardship, imagination and problem-solving skills atrophy. Without adversity, wisdom never can be gained.

The apostle Peter after years in the grist mill of faith says in 1 Peter 4:

> Dear friends, do not be surprised at the painful trial
> you are suffering, as though something strange were
> happening to you. But rejoice that you participate in the
> sufferings of Christ, so that you may be overjoyed when
> his glory is revealed. If you are insulted because of the
> name of Christ, you are blessed, for the Spirit of glory
> and of God rests on you. If you suffer, it should not be
> as a murderer or thief or any other kind of criminal, or
> even as a meddler. However, if you suffer as a Christian,
> do not be ashamed, but praise God that you bear that

name. For it is time for judgment to begin with the
family of God; and if it begins with us, what will the
outcome be for those who do not obey the gospel of
God? (12–17)

What goes on in your mind when you encounter someone who is
incredibly different than you?

This word Peter uses here for "surprise" is the Greek *xenizo*. At
its root it means to show hospitality to strangers. Basically Peter is
trying to get at the core of how we encounter suffering internally.
He comments on how we deal with hardship on a deeply emotional
and cognitive level. His thought is, "As Christians, let's not engage
adversity as if it were a stranger in our midst but as an intrinsic
part of who we are." Why would Peter say this? What is going on
in these Christians' lives that would cause such adversity? Why is
there joy in associating with the suffering of Jesus?

The first-century Christians lived out of a consciousness that
found joy in suffering in Christ because they knew this was an indicator that they were actively participating in his larger covenantal
plan. For, you see, if we follow Christ and follow closely, it is only
natural that some of the adversity he faced will befall us. It is my
job to follow as close to Christ as I can. I want to follow so close,
because if Christ is being glorified, I want in on some of that light.
If Christ is teaching something, I want to be within earshot. Even if
Christ is getting hurt for carrying out his Father's business, I want
the honor of taking a few of the blows that may have missed him.
This is why we have these unique moments in the New Testament
like Acts 5 when the apostles are arrested. Almost immediately after
their arrest, an angel frees them, saying, "Go, stand and speak to
the people in the Temple the whole message of this new Life." Then
word gets back to the authorities that the people they just locked
up are out preaching again. When questioned the apostles say:

"We must obey God rather than men. The God of our fathers raised up Jesus, whom you had put to death by hanging Him on a cross. He is the one whom God exalted to His right hand as a Prince and a Savior, to grant repentance to Israel, and forgiveness of sins. And we are witnesses of these things; and so is the Holy Spirit, whom God has given to those who obey Him." (29–32 NASU)

The chief priest, not knowing what to do, resorts to torture and begins beating the followers of Christ. When they are released, these men and women don't skulk away into the shadows, humiliated by the wounds inflicted by that unjust ruler. They went away "from the presence of the Council, rejoicing that they had been considered worthy to suffer shame for His name" (41 NASU).

This is why we get words such as these from Paul in Philippians 3:

I count all things to be loss in view of the surpassing value of knowing Christ Jesus my Lord, for whom I have suffered the loss of all things, and count them but rubbish so that I may gain Christ, and may be found in Him, not having a righteousness of my own derived from the Law, but that which is through faith in Christ, the righteousness which comes from God on the basis of faith, that I may know Him and the power of His resurrection and the fellowship of His sufferings, being conformed to His death; in order that I may attain to the resurrection from the dead. (8–11 NASB)

In those first days of the church, we see this indomitable belief that adversity was a natural part of life but, more importantly, a part of doing the will of God. It seems as if the prevailing thought process of those in the Way of Christ told them: There is value in enduring adversity. There is a willing endurance of adversity in Christ which can lead us to an expanded capacity to trust.

I am always drawn again and again to the adversity Abraham endured in Genesis 22:1–18. In our time we are so predisposed to comfort instead of adversity. This is one of the insidious side-effects of prosperity. It softens us to the notion of hardship. I found this out once I began a tradition of taking my classes and discipleship groups through an exercise of placing themselves in the shoes of Abraham as he encounters the list of adversities mentioned in this incredible biblical text. I ask people to attempt to feel what he felt and to experience, if only in their imaginations, what this man of faith could possibly have gone through as this narrative unfolds. So I slowly and intimately begin reading the account of what takes place in Genesis 22 where God tests Abraham by asking him to sacrifice his son Isaac. God does this to establish this narrative element of son-sacrifice to prepare everyone for God's own sacrifice of his Son.

So I am reading to a class about how God takes Abraham on this journey that leads to such severe adversity. I typically ask the class to raise their hand when they believe the adversity would become too much for them. As I read, I don't get three verses into the chapter before one hand shoots up. I'm shocked because I haven't gotten to any of the major conflict yet, and already a hand is up, and I am wondering what the adverse condition was that would make this person want to give up so quickly in this encounter. So I stop reading and ask what we just read that would lead them to give up. Their answer? That Abraham had to get up early in the morning, and I'm just not a morning person. We hadn't got to the parts in the passage that talked of Abraham's gathering the tools for his son's demise or dealing with his son's questions or even having to raise a knife to kill his son before God stops him. How many of us would give up if we had to deal with the adversity of just waking up early to begin that harrowing day?

As ghastly as the experience must have been for Abraham, the result is an expanded capacity to trust. Not only that, but after all of the adversity and trying and testing, something beautiful happens at the end of this experience. After all is said and done, what we see is a return to the covenant promise. God says to Abraham, "I will use your life to end this profound sense of alienation in the world." The great Victorian age preacher Charles Spurgeon said once: "I bear willing witness that I owe more to the fire, and the hammer, and the file, than to anything else in my Lord's workshop. I sometimes question whether I have ever learned anything except through the rod. When my schoolroom is darkened, I see most." Beyond the trials that naturally come from life, if we are going to grow spiritually, we are going to have to endure the adversity associated with growth itself. In some sense all spiritual disciplines deal in some way with adversity. When we look at the study of God's word, worshiping God, sitting in silence and solitude, meditating, serving, living a simpler life, all of it requires a sacrifice of time. This is especially true in an event-rich and time-starved culture like ours. The study of God's word requires a wrestling with truths counter to the prevailing thoughts of the day. There is adversity in reading the Bible, often because it places an unflattering mirror up to my face, when I am all too familiar with denial instead of the stark reality that is being thrust before me. There is adversity when the veil is stripped from me, only to highlight how small the relevance of my life is when sometimes I want it to just be about me, my family, and my stuff. There is profound adversity in the reading and studying of God's word.

To sit in silence and meditation requires us to deal with the adversity of our distracted minds. Silence requires us to see ourselves as we are. Doing without, whatever it might be, is

uncomfortable, whether sitting in silence or denying our crea-
ture comforts. Intrinsic in fasting is this built-in struggle we must
embrace if there is any hope of growth. One of the biggest challenges we will have to face if we commit to change and transformation is building margin into our lives to make the time to
participate in those disciplines and activities that grow us. To say
yes to growth and development is to say no to other things that
take up way too much time and offer far too little growth. To
create margin in our lives and say no to those time-drains drives
us headlong into adversity. It hurts sometimes to pull away from
things that stunt our growth.

The great painter Timanthes bears witness to this truth. Well
over two-thousand years ago, Timanthes mastered his craft under
a wise and insightful tutor. Timanthes's tutor poured his life and
understanding of painting into his young pupil. After several years,
all of his mentoring and care for his student birthed an amazing
painting. Timanthes painted the greatest piece of art work he had
ever produced. He was so proud and pleased by his own effort
that he spent countless hours staring at his painting. Struck by its
beauty, the young painter studied every brush stroke he had used.
He marveled at the colors that had blossomed from his brush and
the subtle hues he was able to capture on this canvas. He spent days
staring at his painting. Then one morning when he entered the
studio in preparation to spend more time marveling at his hand-
iwork, Timanthes found every inch of his coveted work daubed
and blotted with smears of paint. Furious, the young artist ran
to his teacher to question him about the desecration of his work.
His teacher was happy to admit that he had destroyed the young
man's painting. He was reported to have said, "I did it for your
own good. That painting was retarding your progress." Timanthes,
struck by his teacher's words, continued to grow. He continued to

learn. Then, soon afterward, he painted the *Sacrifice of Iphigenia*, which is regarded as one of the greatest masterpieces of antiquity.

We don't pursue adversity. We don't attempt to track down suffering and despair. Troubles are part of the warp and woof of life lived. So if adversity cannot be avoided, maybe it can be utilized. Perhaps the traumatic experiences of life can become the shaping tools God uses on us as we lie as living sacrifices on his sacred altar. The only problem with living sacrifices is that they move. God can only use our adversities if we are willing to engage them instead of avoiding or running away from them, and this requires a thing called adherence.

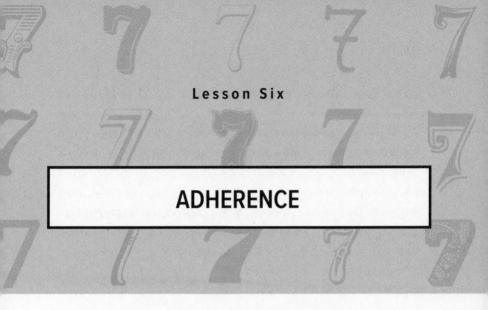

Lesson Six

ADHERENCE

*Your level of growth is commensurate
with the length of your endurance.*

I WAS OVERWHELMED BY ONE PARTICULAR EVENT DURING THE Gentlemen's Singles tournament of the 2010 Wimbledon Championships. The twenty-third seed, American John Isner, began a seemingly typical match with French qualifier Nicolas Mahut. The match began at 6:13 P.M. on a Tuesday. As the tennis match continued, the players were tied at two sets each. Wimbledon rules state that there can be no tie-breaker in the decisive fifth set; the players must win by two games. So they played on. At 9:10 P.M. the line judge called the game because it was just too dark. The game resumed the next day at 2:05 P.M. The men played game after game, ace after ace, volley after volley, until 9:10 P.M. that Wednesday night. The game was called again due to darkness. Play resumed the next day at 3:43 P.M. Isner finally closed out the victory with a backhand passing shot, then collapsed on his back as he tossed his racket in jubilation and relief at 4:48 P.M. These men played the longest match in tennis history, measured both by time and the number of games—eleven hours, five minutes of play over three days, with a total of one-hundred eighty-three games played. Imagine the toll on their bodies, their emotions, and their wills. What allowed them to continue? If these two men can teach us anything, it would be our sixth lesson of faith, which is adherence:

> *Your level of growth is commensurate with the length of your endurance.*

Scripture has a lot to say about the idea of adherence—our ability to stick and stay with and in a trying situation. More than eighty references appear in the New Testament alone discussing endurance, perseverance, and bearing up under certain situations. Jesus has this on his mind as he teaches the parable of sowing seed. You will remember why the seed sown on rocky ground does not grow. "Others, like seed sown on rocky places, hear the word and at once receive it with joy. But since they have no root, they last only a short time. When trouble or persecution comes because of the word, they quickly fall away" (Mark 4:16–17).

Biblical Examples of Adherence

Jesus's life alone is a testament of adherence and endurance. Away from his Father, encased in flesh, Jesus spends thirty years in preparation for three glorious years of ministry. When it comes to adherence, I am always mindful of Anna in the New Testament, seemingly a footnote in Jesus's birth narrative, but one of the great examples of staying in a condition—a circumstance—waiting for her moment in the Jesus story.

And there was a prophetess, Anna the daughter of
Phanuel, of the tribe of Asher. She was advanced in
years and had lived with her husband seven years after
her marriage, and then as a widow to the age of eighty-
four. She never left the temple, serving night and day
with fasting and prayers. At that very moment she came
up and began giving thanks to God, and continued
to speak of Him to all those who were looking for the
redemption of Jerusalem. (Luke 2:36–38 NASB)

That is adherence.

Jesus's brother James makes adherence a key component in
how he sees and understands growth. He says in James 1:2–4,
"Consider it all joy, my brethren, when you encounter various trials,
knowing that the testing of your faith produces endurance. And let
endurance have its perfect result, so that you may be perfect and
complete, lacking in nothing." This command is for us to have a
sense of complete or whole joy during the hardest times. How do
you tend to look at trials in your life? Is joy the first thing that comes
to mind? There would have to be a major paradigm shift for that
to occur. Right? The thought is this: we will see trials as a means
of complete or whole joy if we come to understand what God is
doing to the believer during those trials. God's ardent desire for you
is for you to possess something the Greeks called *hypomone*. This
word in the original context means steadfastness, staying power,
constancy, adherence. Here we are not talking about a one-time
event where you held strong. Instead we are talking about your interior nature, your very character shaped by *hypomone*. This word
describes who you are—a person whose very nature exemplifies
steadfastness and consistency. The gift of *hypomone* is just getting
the ball rolling. Once you possess *hypomone*, it breeds *telios*. As
James says in his next verse, "Let endurance have its perfect result,

so that you may be perfect and complete, lacking in nothing." *Telos* is a key term in James. No other New Testament book uses it more often. When it describes character, it implies that God is a part of whatever process is involved in the formation of your character. It is eschatological in its focus—which means that you can become a person of integrity, single-minded in loyalty and devotion to God, a fully developed character of stability in God's eternal plan.

This idea of perfection has its roots in an Old Testament concept characterized by two Hebrew words, *tamim* and *shalem*. *Tamim* means blameless, innocent, sound, wholesome, unimpaired, having integrity; it describes what is complete or entirely in accord with truth and fact. *Shalem* means to be complete, safe, peaceful, perfect, whole, full, at peace, perfect, and most importantly, finished. None of this can occur without *hypomone*—without adherence. Paul says it this way in Romans 5:

> Therefore, having been justified by faith, we have peace with God through our Lord Jesus Christ, through whom also we have obtained our introduction by faith into this grace in which we stand; and we exult in hope of the glory of God. And not only this, but we also exult in our tribulations, knowing that tribulation brings about perseverance; and perseverance, proven character; and proven character, hope; and hope does not disappoint, because the love of God has been poured out within our hearts through the Holy Spirit who was given to us. For while we were still helpless, at the right time Christ died for the ungodly. For one will hardly die for a righteous man; though perhaps for the good man someone would dare even to die. But God demonstrates His own love toward us, in that while we were yet sinners, Christ died for us. (1–8 NASU)

Adherence under Spiritual Disciplines

It is vitally important for us to have endurance and stick-to-it-iveness in life. It becomes especially important as it relates to engaging in spiritual disciplines.

Most of these spiritual disciplines have immediate effect on the body and spirit of a person. Positive long-term changes also occur when we are persistent in these exercises. As a matter of fact, scientists have found that positive long-term effects on the body and brain come through persistent engagement versus sporadic engagement in spiritual disciplines.

Prayer and Meditation

There is a powerful reason Paul tells us in 1 Thessalonians 5:17 to "pray without ceasing." Scientists and researchers have found that if a person prays and meditates consistently over a long period of time, the practice affects cortisol levels in the body.

Cortisol is a hormone. It is a vital, helpful part of the body's response to stress. In the stressful world we live in much of the time, cortisol is coursing through our bodies all of the time. Higher and more prolonged levels of cortisol in the bloodstream (such as those associated with chronic stress) have been shown to have such negative effects as impaired cognitive performance, suppressed thyroid function, blood sugar imbalances such as hyperglycemia, decreased bone density, decrease in muscle tissue, high blood-pressure, lowered immunity, and depression.

Long-term commitment to prayer and meditation has the ability to reduce levels of cortisol.

Bible Study

James 1:25 says, "He who looks into the perfect law of liberty and continues in it, and is not a forgetful hearer but a doer of the word, this one will be blessed in what he does" (NKJV).

Have you ever wondered how information we take in moves from being just information—to belief—and then to action? When information comes in, it is stored in a part of the brain called the hippocampus. When the word of God is preached or taught to us, this is where that information is stored. The hippocampus is only for short-term memory use. Information stored in this region of the brain can only be accessed for two to four weeks.

Continual study causes the information stored in the hippocampus to move. As we sit with information, ruminate, and ponder thoughts, this information moves from short-term storage to the cerebral cortex. (What's interesting to note is that the cerebral cortex is where belief also is stored.) The cerebral cortex then engages the other parts of the limbic system where choices are made. Adherence to study enables information to migrate to a place where that information can actually have long-term impact on an individual's life. Critical information journeys to a place where it can be transformed into belief, which, in turn, becomes behavior and action.

Does this peek inside our cranium help you to see the importance of sticking with prayer, sticking with study?

Developing Adherence

Experience in this field shows us that adherence can be developed. We do not have to function as those who give up. God uniquely designed us as beings who have the ability to stick and stay. As a matter of fact, God is the source of our adherence. Romans 15:5 actually states that it is "God who gives perseverance and encouragement" (NASU)—God and his indwelling Spirit.

Adherence becomes a reasonable response to our relationship with God when we realize that all we do is connected to God's larger redemptive plan. We find over and over in Scripture that what we do as followers of Christ, while sometimes thankless and seemingly irrelevant, is not done in vain, as 1 Corinthians 15:58 reminds us.

A dear friend recently told me a story about a person she met at church. She felt compelled to visit this new acquaintance. Of course, as often is the case, reticence kicked in. Doubts began to flood her resolve. A barrage of perfectly good excuses came to mind to prevent her from doing what her heart had been called to complete. Resisting the gravitational pull of all her misgivings, however, she moved. She went to this person's work, a local restaurant, and, although clumsy and hesitant, she spent five minutes touching base, in the place-your-order line, with her new friend. Unbeknown to the lady who told me this story, those five minutes meant the world to this person she contacted in that cafe. Burdened with the guilt of her past, the young lady behind the counter felt that no one at a church would want to have anything to do with her. But she found out she was wrong. Right there before her was the face of a Christian who was willing to break through the guilt to get to a person in desperate need of a lifeline.

Often we think the things we strain to do for God may be foolish and sometimes futile, but these may turn out to be the very things that change the trajectory of someone in powerful ways. Regardless of their outcome, our efforts are tied to something and to Someone bigger than the moment of effort itself. The fleeting moments of our action may be the result of eternal planning and may have eternal results. When we grasp the significance of our actions, it can breed a greater sense of adherence.

Another great booster to adherence is coming to an understanding that what we do as Christians has great intrinsic value. "Intrinsic value" can be defined as an activity that is connected to the core of who we are. An activity has intrinsic value when it has value in and of itself. It's worth doing just because it's worth doing, whether you get anything out of it besides doing the activity itself. Despite any and all residual benefits, an activity with intrinsic value is worth doing just because at its core it has meaning in the doing itself.

Self-Determination Theory (SDT) capitalizes on this notion of intrinsic value. Researchers have studied and found a link between intrinsic value and adherence. SDT theorists have been looking at the "why" behind people's commitment to an activity. They ask, for example, why do some people stick to a workout regimen and others don't? They are looking at what is at work in human behavior that would allow some to succeed in developing and maintaining healthy habits, while others cannot. What they have found is that the more self-determined we are—that is, the more we're doing what we want to do and aren't being forced to do—the happier and more successful we tend to be. In case you're wondering, external rewards and punishments may influence our behavior, but we are also driven to do things simply for their own sake. That's the nature of intrinsic motivation—it's something that, from a psychological point of view, is done for its own sake. If we like doing the activity for the sake of the activity, we tend to continue doing it much longer. If we work out to look good for someone else, that is an extrinsic motivator, and typically this is not a long-lasting motivator. If we find an exercise that we like doing purely for the sake of doing it, we tend to adhere to the practice for much longer stents. So the question is: what makes us like doing an activity?

A number of factors make us like doing a thing. Here are just a few.

- We like doing an activity if we feel that we made the choice to do it. This is called autonomy. If we feel forced into an activity, we tend to reject it, regardless of its intrinsic value.

- We also like an activity if we feel that we have a sense of competency in it. If we feel that we have a handle on the activity, we tend to adhere to it much longer than if we feel we are incapable.
- Another element which causes us to like an activity is relatedness. If the activity in some way causes us to connect to others who enjoy the same activity, we tend to stick with it longer.

This is magnificent information to know as we look at our spiritual life and growth. There is so much to learn and apply here.

Take kids and worship as an example. Too often as children we feel like we are forced to participate in worship. We hear far too many stories of kids being dragged to church on Sunday morning. Because of the forced nature of the encounter, many young people are put off by something that should be a part of the very fabric of their being. Worship is as natural as breathing. To be in the Presence of the divine and rehearse with him all of his attributes—not for his sake but for ours—is joy. That is, unless a person feels as if her autonomy is snatched away in the process.

Our competence in spiritual disciplines is always a part of our engagement with them, especially in prayer. I believe we have more worries about prayer than actual prayers themselves.

- Am I doing it right?
- Am I praying enough?
- Did I use the right words?
- Did I do it long enough?
- Is God even listening?

All of these questions chip away at our competence in this matter, but I believe these questions are birthed from a place of socially or self-imposed judgment.

Prayer, along with many other spiritual disciplines, is not a skill to master but a relationship to embrace. Prayer, worship, silence, study, and even fasting are all steps toward deeper relationship. It is often religious institutions and our own judgmental voices that turn these acts of relationship into a punishment/reward activity. If you are praying, you are doing it right. Success or failure aside, your attempt to engage God is met with loving acceptance, because this is who our God is. Certainly we do see in the Bible many participating in prayer and fasting and even acts of generosity for selfish and self-aggrandizing reasons. Certainly such motivation has never and will never impress God. But if we are humbly and sincerely coming to God, offering our time-worn and meager efforts to connect with him, God receives it as any father would receive such efforts.

The more we are gracious with ourselves and see our competency in these disciplines, and the more we see the intrinsic value in our unique relationship with God, the more we begin to like these activities. The more we like them for what they are, the longer will be our adherence in these activities. And the longer we can stay on the altar of these activities, the more we can offer up ourselves to God for him to forever change us.

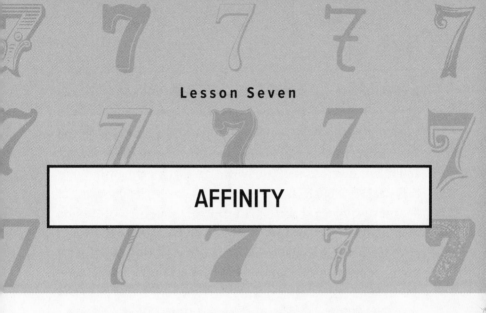

AFFINITY

*Your level of spiritual growth is commensurate with
the healthy people with whom you surround yourself.*

I F YOU WERE A CHILD OR IF YOU RAISED CHILDREN FROM THE
late '60s on, you will remember *Sesame Street*. This was such a
ground-breaking show. They took the notion of education and
growth seriously. They made painstaking efforts to do whatever
they could to insure the effective education and growth of their
young viewers.

I remember being enthralled by every image and every scene
they showed. I remember each character and every song I heard,
even to this day. One of the songs they sang all through the show's
history was "Who Are the People in Your Neighborhood?" The
song was written by the Emmy-award-winning head writer of the
show. He wrote it to teach kids about the influence people have
in our lives by the things they do. The Sesame characters would

sing about the janitor, the night watchman, or the weatherman, all the people you meet when you're walking down the street. You are connected to them in some way. They have influence on you. They impact your life. If you just take the time to think about it and reflect, the idea was, you would see that seemingly insignificant people we often take for granted have major influence in our lives. If you just step back a little bit to gain some perspective, you discover that everyone you are affiliated with shapes some aspect of your life. What would we do without the grocer's clerk? What would life be like without the police officer or the teacher who, due to familiarity, seem to garner little attention but in fact plays a sizeable role in who you are and how you function?

The lesson of affinity asks you to consider who those people are in your neighborhood and how much influence they have in your spiritual life and development. The lesson of affinity states,

> *Your level of spiritual growth is commensurate with the healthy people with whom you surround yourself.*

I love the thoughts Norie Huddle shares in her children's book about butterflies. She says the caterpillar's new cells are called "imaginal cells." They resonate at a different frequency than his old ones. They are so totally different from the caterpillar cells that his immune system thinks they are enemies and gobbles them up—Chomp! Gulp! But these new imaginal cells continue to appear. More and more of them! Pretty soon the caterpillar's immune system cannot destroy them fast enough. More and more of the imaginal cells survive. And then an amazing thing happens. The little, tiny, lonely imaginal cells start to clump together into friendly little groups. They all resonate together at the same frequency, passing information from one to another. Then, after a while, another amazing thing happens. The clumps of imaginal cells start to cluster together—into a long string of clumping and clustering imaginal cells, all resonating at the same frequency, all passing information from one to another there inside the chrysalis. A wave of Good News travels throughout the system. It lurches and heaves . . . but that clump is not yet a butterfly. Then at some point, the entire long string of imaginal cells suddenly realizes all together that it is Something Different from the caterpillar. Something New! Something Wonderful! With that realization comes the shout of the birth of the butterfly. Since the butterfly now "knows" it is a butterfly, the little tiny imaginal cells no longer have to do all those things individual cells have to do. Now they are part of a multi-celled organism—*a family* who can share the work. Each new butterfly cell can take on a different job. There is something for everyone to do. Everyone is important. Each cell begins to do just that exact thing it is most drawn to do. Every other cell encourages it to do just that. What a great way to organize a butterfly!

The Creation Model

As we noted previously, in the beginning was a "We"—a divine and glorious "We" who existed in pure and unadulterated union. In the beginning was community, and there was healthy community. God the Father, God the Son and God the Holy Spirit functioned in union with one another. This union was one of indivisibility and uniqueness of individual-ness at the same time.

From start to finish in Scripture we see this amazing symphony of mutual connectedness and deference. It's as if God, Christ, and God's own Spirit are deferring to one another's right of sovereignty. Each aspect of "Godness" is cheering on the other as they each watch the other aspect of Deity carry out that Person's intended function—each one celebrating and making way for the other to be extraordinary in his own right. This is seen clearly when Jesus constantly affirms that his message does not come from himself, but he only preaches what God has told him to proclaim. In a moment of great passion and power, Jesus says it is better for him to leave Earth so the Holy Spirit can come. Jesus thought it so important to make room for the other portion of his divine partnership that he would choose to leave the people he loves. That is deference at its best. All through history God has been making room for God. God has cut a path for God. They keep facilitating the success of one another as they seek to execute the purpose they set out to achieve before time began.

Creation was this amazing compassionate invitation into the community and oneness that they had for eternity. As believers, we are invited into a powerful cosmology. "Cosmology" describes all of the active participants in a particular space and time. To understand cosmology is to ask the question: Who are the people in your neighborhood? Who are the ones that have influence in your decision making and your behavior? In the Christian cosmology you have several seen and unseen participants who ought to impact your decision making and behaviors. Our Christian community itself should ideally have influence in who we are and what we are about. Ideally, as we make decisions, we ask what positive or negative impact each decision will have on our community of believers. When I am about to encourage someone at school, when I am about to come to someone's defense on the job, when I am about to tell or listen to this dirty joke at the water cooler, when I am about to gossip on the phone: if we are in fact a "we," that decision can positively or negatively impact us all.

The fact that we sometimes forget to acknowledge our cosmological connection with one another makes it so much easier to fall into sin. We feel like the stakes aren't really that high because the impact seems localized. But sin impacts the whole camp. One of the moments in Scripture that I hate the most but see as absolutely telling is that time outside the gates of Jericho in Joshua 6. God had given Joshua and his armies the most unorthodox plan to destroy a heavily walled city. Play music. Blow horns. March around the gates with the Ark of the Covenant, and they will be destroyed. The command also included:

> Keep away from the devoted things, so that you will
> not bring about your own destruction by taking any of
> them. Otherwise you will make the camp of Israel liable
> to destruction and bring trouble on it. All the silver and
> gold and the articles of bronze and iron are sacred to the
> LORD and must go into his treasury. (Josh. 6:18–19)

Whatever was plundered from the victory was to be set aside for God. "Lest we think this battle was about us and our own tenacity, let's devote everything we find to the One who secured for us the win," Joshua tells his soldiers. "Let everything be devoted to God." This worked fine for everyone except one soldier. One man in the camp, a guy named Achan, never considered the impact of his greed. Due to Achan's greed, the whole army was out of sync with God, and because they were out of sync, the tiny army of the seemingly insignificant town of Ai defeated the Israelite army. Achan's fellow-soldiers fell because of his inability to see that his shortcomings affected them all.

Just as there is no such thing as a victimless sin, so too are there no localized sins. So much impact comes from the sins we commit. Everything is so interconnected in our world. My shortcomings reverberate beyond my soul and impact my world. At the moment when any one of us is out of sync with God, we lose the opportunity.

The very act of creation itself is a model of this law. In Genesis 1:26 God says, "Let Us make man in Our image" (NASU). In the beginning was community, and in the beginning was healthy community. There before the beginning of time were God, Jesus, and the Holy Spirit functioning from this sacred, healthy place of affinity. All through the Bible we see this divine community functioning together and having profound influence with and in one another.

Before there was earth and sky, there was the very Spirit of God hovering over what was yet to be formed—the Spirit of God hovering over possibility, waiting with bated anticipation over potential, over what could be. Later in Colossians we find that Jesus was there as well, functioning as the causal agent of creation. God spoke, Jesus performed, and the Spirit stood as a caring witness to what was to be.

The creation of humanity was an act, an outpouring of affection and intimacy between and amongst this sacred "Us." Much like a married couple whose love spills over to such a degree that the only way to express that love is to have a child to share it with, this divine "Us" needed a way to capture what their love for one another really meant. So much so that creation itself became an invitation to join this sacred and healthy community. Then all of a sudden the "let Us" turned into a "let them." Let them be a part of this process of creation and of making the most of life and love. The very moment God looked over what he had accomplished within this healthy community, he said it was more than good, that it was very good. Without a doubt it was, and much of it still is very good, because we, as those who have accepted the invitation, are ushered into a vast and unique cosmology. Then Hebrews 12:1 tells us that those believers who have come before us ideally have influence on us. "Since we have so great a cloud of witnesses surrounding us," this verse counsels, "let us also lay aside every encumbrance and the sin which so easily entangles us, and let us run with endurance the race that is set before us" (NASB).

Here the writer is picturing a race that we are in. And as we look into the stands, who do we see? All those faithful believers who have died and now are cheering us on. I imagine Abraham there, nodding his head in affirmation in those moments when we take steps into the unknown with questionable faith but a willingness to go. I image him nodding his head emphatically saying, "Yes, I know what that feels like. But keep going. There are blessings on the other side of this test!" I see Moses and Caleb cheering you on as you deal with the difficulties of transitioning from one status to another. Both of them in chorus say, "Keep going! Regardless of how many fail or fall around you, keep believing and keep running." Mary the mother of Jesus is in the stands. She sees you pondering the joys and pains of the journey, and she says, "Run, and don't forget all of the joys and all of the heartache. This makes the run richer." All of the saints of the past who finished the race you are still running are in the stands, celebrating each step you take, knowing the difficulty but also cognizant of the prize that awaits you.

At the center of this Christian cosmology is Christ. I learned this in a really significant way two years into my ministry. With great optimism and naïveté, I wanted to send out a letter to all of the churches in the surrounding area to let them know about the ministry work we were doing in our congregation. The church secretary, much wiser and more seasoned in ministry than I, asked me what churches I wanted to send these letters to. I started preaching this sermon in the middle of the office about the oneness of the church and how we all have to participate in the healing and helping of the people we were serving. She listened with the patience and love of a mother who had heard enough tantrums not to be shaken by another one. After the sermon was through, she pulled out a phone book and showed me the fractured nature not only of all the churches in the area but of those in our specific tribe— all of the churches that were divided because of one insignificant tradition after the other, divided by race, practice, and tradition. She said, "Now, Eric, I want to ask you again . . . which churches do you want me to send this to?"

I caught myself stumbling back into my office, shaken by the blow of reality I had just absorbed. With so many fractured ties, what could I hinge my ministry on? If not the church itself, what could be the center point of my faith and work? So I literally cleared my theological table of everything I once believed and used to come to blows about and started with a clean slate. From that moment on, I placed Christ at the center of all things and began to rebuild a theology, my understanding of the Bible, and the sum total of my work, with Christ at the center of all things. It did wonders for my ministry, but it did even more for my life.

If we are all alone in this attempt to grasp and live in this Kingdom consciousness, we are doomed. The race is too long and the distractions that seek to destroy our mindfulness are far too great. But, if we are surrounded by a powerful cosmology that seeks to guide and encourage every step of this impossible task, then all of a sudden the task becomes very possible.

The key to our success is making sure that our group of others is a healthy affinity group. 1 Corinthians 15:33 warns, "Do not be misled: 'Bad company corrupts good character.'" We are shaped by our affinity groups. While speaking to one men's group, I stated, "Men are shaped in the company of other men. If you want to make sure your son grows up to be a decent, God-honoring man, the best thing you can do is to surround him by decent, God-honoring men. It will be the only thing he sees to model." The same is true for girls. The same is true for disciples. The same is true for Christians in general. To grow Christians, you must ensure they are surrounded by good healthy Christians. The same is true in a negative sense as well. If we invite people into our churches and they are placed among consumers instead of disciples, they will begin to believe that church is all about their needs instead of the mission and vision of Jesus Christ.

Characteristics of a Healthy Affinity Group

Here is a list of characteristics that mark a healthy affinity group. These are characteristics that are present in healthy churches, healthy families, and healthy groups of friends. These characteristics are the key to growth and development in these various groups as well.

Actively Pursuing Individual and Group Growth

If we are to grow, we have to be surrounded by people who are in the midst of growth themselves. Let us never lose sight of the universal truth that life begets life. Growth and development are contagious.

People who are growing and developing provide for us a model and a motivation for our own growth. Surrounding ourselves with these growing people is extremely helpful, especially if they are pursuing not only their growth but the growth of others. You know those people in your life. You are familiar with those who ask the challenging questions that foster deeper thoughts. You know those people who speak words of encouragement to you at just the right time. It is critically important that we people our environment with individuals who believe in us and our potential. If you look around your landscape and find yourself lacking associates like this, you know what needs to be one of the first things on your to-do list. It is time to pray for and pursue healthy additions to your community.

Accountability

King David in the Old Testament was known as a man after God's own heart. He pursued a deep and abiding relationship with God, and God pursued a similar relationship with him. David was tasked to build a great nation and serve as catalyst for the future Kingdom of Christ. This was a heavy burden to bear for one so flawed and prone to fail. David's saving grace was the fact that God placed other men in his life to hold him accountable for the profound failings that occurred in his life. One of David's accountability partners was Nathan.

Nathan walked with David through the whole Bathsheba scandal. While David's lust led to infidelity and murder, misbehavior he might have gotten away with due to his power and influence, God and his friend Nathan refused to allow this sin to destroy him. Nathan came to King David and loved him enough to risk his own life to confront him. To a man vested with limitless power, a man who had killed wild beasts and a giant Philistine and an innocent soldier, Nathan came and dared to confront him about the sins David thought he had got away with. It wouldn't have been that difficult for David to add one more murder to the heap in order to avoid addressing this sin. So Nathan was literally risking it all to confront a friend. He did it by telling the king a made-up story about a wealthy man taking a poor man's only sheep to feed a traveling stranger. David was furious and demanded yet another death, only to find out that Nathan was talking about his offense of taking Bathsheba. Because of Nathan's courage and his wise words, David repented and found himself closer to God instead of estranged.

It is so important for all of us to have "Nathans" in our lives. If we are going to grow, we need key people to love us enough not just to say what we want to hear but what we need to hear. We have to have those men and women in our lives who know us well enough to say what needs to be said, and to say it in ways where we can truly hear truth. There are far too many stories of powerful men and women who, to their own detriment, surround themselves with sycophants who parrot the yes which pleases the ear but not the no that truly grows the human heart. To have a Nathan in your affinity group is to have an invaluable aid to your growth and transformation.

Ownership Culture vs. Blame

I would love to believe I have a level of maturity that has unmoored itself from all of my childhood hang-ups and notions. One sign of true maturity is a frankness that admits, as Langston Hughes would say, how beautiful and ugly we are. One of the ugly aspects of my walk is that I never want to be seen as the bad boy. I don't want to be the one caught with his hand in the cookie jar. I don't want to be the one facing the reprimand of my father or the fussing of my mother. But let me be even more honest—I still want the unwarranted cookie in the jar. I still want to do the bad stuff that deserves the reprimand. I just want to frame the offense in the way that makes it seem as though I am still a good boy.

What this paradox has created inside me is a tendency to blame others for my behaviors and choices people don't approve of. This tendency gets me entry into one of the largest clubs around. The culture club of blame welcomes me with open arms. As long as I'm willing to justify my maladaptive behaviors by drawing attention to others' behaviors, I will always be accepted. There will always be a vacant seat I can occupy among the blame culture. The very moment I begin seeing my actions for what they are, I'm no longer fit for their fellowship. When I take responsibility for my sin and my sinful decisions, I'm no longer welcome among the blamers. Now I am fit to enter into healthy community.

Healthy community says, "It was me. I did it. You caught me red-handed." Healthy community demands that all the people in the circle own up to their stuff. Healthy community no longer accepts the fiction that everyone else is to blame for your bad behavior and sinful decisions, because healthy community wants to stay healthy. Denial and blame offer temporary solace but never long-term growth. Blame makes it incumbent upon others to fix my ills by adjusting their character.

Healthy community welcomes those who take ownership of their shortcomings and their role in the development process, and those in the healthy circle can take ownership of their stuff because the circle holds a rich understanding of God's grace. They have learned and believe that the sacrifice that delights God is a broken spirit and a contrite heart. That's the disposition God loves and accepts. It becomes the type of heart God can truly work with to transform. If we want to grow, we are going to have to surround ourselves with people like this, people who take ownership of their fallenness as well as taking ownership for their portion of the responsibility to grow.

Emotional Health

It is also critically incumbent upon us all to surround ourselves with people who are emotionally healthy. While dealing with someone physically unhealthy, Jesus asked an important question. He encountered a lame man who was surrounded by other sick people. All of them were relying on the possible power of a healing pool called Bethesda. Jesus asked the man, "Do you want to be healed?" Is this something you actually want? Jesus asked him. Do you want this transformation to actually occur? This is a pertinent question to ask. However, instead of answering it, upon hearing the question, the man gave all of the reasons he couldn't get into the pool of water at just the right time. Everyone believed an angel would stir up the pool and thereby facilitate the healing of the first person who made it to the water.

"What?! Did you not hear the question?" I want to yell at the lame man through the recesses of time. Didn't you hear the question Jesus just asked you? It wasn't why haven't you been healed, but do you *want* to be healed? The lame man was basing his healing on the possibility that other sick people might grab him and throw him into the pool in time for the healing to take place. Jesus's question still hangs thick in the air. Is health something you really want?

That lame man could not be healed because he was relying on other sick people in his environment to offer help. Sadly, unhealthy people seldom have the strength to help others, because they are always busy healing themselves. I believe this is true with physical health and emotional health as well.

The emotionally healthy must be a key part of our affinity groups if we plan to grow. We want to surround ourselves with people who, while they may not have worked through all of their issues and concerns, have taken large leaps in assuring their own emotional health. We want to take the necessary steps to ensure that we have begun to deal with our own brokenness enough so that we can be healthy emotional resources to others. This does not mean we shouldn't reach out to those who are broken. Most certainly we receive comfort from God so that we can comfort those by the comfort we have received. That's biblical. I believe we find a sense of healing when we help other people heal, but these people who so desperately need healing are not those you should include in your affinity group. Your affinity group should be made up of those who are emotionally mature enough to foster mutual growth and development into Christlikeness.

Communication

Heathy groups communicate in healthy ways. They speak from the deepest parts of their hearts, and they listen to the deepest parts of yours. Healthy groups communicate in a way that builds up and never attempts to tear down.

I know a family whose commitment to one another is unparalleled. They would do anything for each other at the drop of a hat or at the first sign of need. They love each other and have proved it on countless occasions. But you wouldn't know this by the way they communicate with one another. They speak out of anger, crisis, and conflict. Body language and tone suggest bitterness, distance, and downright animosity. I heard them argue once about how one of them had said, "How are you?" The response to the greeting was, "Why did you ask me like that?" The tirade escalated into high-pitched tones of impatience. My pulse quickened until I realized that this is just the way they communicate. They have never functioned from a place of healthy communication.

Truth be told, too few of us function with healthy communication styles. One of the reasons for this is because healthy communication is seldom modeled. We certainly don't see healthy communication styles modeled for us on the television shows we see or the movies we watch. Of course, the plots of most television shows and movie narratives revolve around some kind of crisis. While dealing with crisis drives a movie plot along and works really well, it doesn't work in our real lives. Modeling our communication styles from the media typically gets us what it gets the main characters in films—more crises. Showing understanding, listening first and speaking afterward, using words that edify rather than tear down would ruin a good movie, but this kind of wise speech brings life to real-life relationships. Why? Because healthy communication strategies ramp down conflict and crisis and facilitate harmony. Once again, that's terrible for movies, but it works wonders for our relationships. This is why it is so important that our affinity groups be filled with healthy communicators.

So the critical question to ask yourself is this: Who are the people in your neighborhood? Who are the people you surround yourself with who aid you in your spiritual growth and whom you help with theirs? We all know the friend who happily invites you into the time-draining stuff of spiritual immobility. We know them, and periodically we need to take the time to name them for who they are. These are friends and family members who are significant parts of our lives, but they must not and cannot have a front-row seat in the performance which is your life of growth. Those whose very presence models the growth we desire and lovingly challenges us to become who God has determined us to be are the people we must intentionally surround ourselves with. Who are the people in your neighborhood, the people you meet when you are walking down your spiritual street?

GETTING BACK ON TRACK

IT WAS ALL GOING SO WELL FOR THE JAPANESE MARATHON runner Natsuki Terada in the Tokyo-Hakone relay race. Along with so many other marathoners, this young man disciplined his body for the rigor of the race. Along with his body, the heart and the mind of the runner were conditioned for the miles ahead. Now, after two days of a 217.9 km grueling test of endurance and strength, Natsuki was coming to the end of his race, with the finish line so close it called to him. This young man was able to muster a final burst of energy to sprint ahead of the other runners. "Not far, not far, not far," every footfall told him as they hit the pavement. That is, until he managed to lose the lead and the race when he took a wrong turn just two hundred meters before the finish line. He got distracted by a nearby camera truck that turned a corner, and he followed it completely off the course.

Almost there, but taken off track.

I think this characterizes moments in my life as it relates to my spiritual growth and maturity in faith. This is a picture of so many of our lives and of the lives of those who follow Christ when it comes to our efforts toward growth and development. We are in the race, and yet somehow we get distracted and find ourselves way off course as it relates to our maturation process in the Lord. The distractions are just too many to number—everything from material possessions to our own blasted egos. Distractions so easily get us off course.

Okay, the good news is this: the young runner got back on course and was able to finish the race. He finished tenth, which qualified him to race again another day. My prayer for myself and for y'all is that we intentionally put those things in our lives that give us the ability to continue in the race. My aim in this book has been to provide a list of elements we can apply to our spiritual walk that will at least allow us to stay on the path of embracing Christlikeness and deeper faith. This is why I have been honored to share with you these seven responses to God's love and right-eousness—these lessons that I see at play in Scripture and in the lives of believers, lessons that promote and foster real substantive growth in all facets of life.

I have been teaching these lessons of faith in classes, in con-ferences, and with those I sit with as a spiritual director. These encounters have been as rich as they were varied. I've shared these seven lessons with athletes and business leaders. I've shared these ideas with stay-at-home moms and with artists. Their enthusiastic response and the strides they have made in their spiritual walk have fueled my ability to finish this writing. I've often felt this information was dated, insignificant, or something said already by far more talented people. That is, until I share these concepts again with someone and see the light of recognition flash in their eyes, as if they have just heard a truth they had always known but could not name. I then receive a new sense of confidence and obligation to continue teaching and writing down these ideas.

The funny thing about my process has been that I've been so focused on exploring the effectiveness of these spiritual truths that I did not see what God was doing. It took a student to show me. After completing a thirteen-week course on these seven principles, an older friend of mine said, "Eric, do you know what you have done?" My thought was, "Yes, finished a class, which means I can move to the next thing on my to-do list for the day." But, having a feeling that this was not what he was talking about, I stood silent, hoping not to expose my cynicism, and positioned myself to listen deeply. He said, "Eric, I don't know if this was your intent or not, but you have laid out a pretty clear-cut process to Christian discipleship. Each one of these things you have referred to is a mile-marker that must be reached if one is to fully embrace living out the ways and teachings of Jesus Christ." I was floored by not having seen what was there the entire time. I scanned quickly through these seven lessons and immediately gained a light grasp of what my friend was telling me. In the following months, and with a greater degree of understanding about this lost Christian art of being and making disciples, I gained an even stronger grasp of what my friend had shared. Yes, God. You were giving us not only a means of growing our faith but a path to take in order to get there!

If we are going to walk this path of faith in an effort to become fully realized disciples of Jesus Christ, inculcating and living out the ways and teachings of our Master, we are going to have to start from a place of *incredulity*. From a place of incredulity, we are launched into a level of *intentionality* that we may have never reached before. When we reach that level, we will have to rid ourselves of some things, which is *abdication*. Simultaneously we dive into something, which is *immersion*. Once we do these things, there is a natural effect that becomes unavoidable—*encountering adversity*. Adversity necessitates a response of *adherence* in the face of that adversity. The only way we can reach any of these mile-markers is to surround ourselves with *healthy people* who become our affinity group.

Now the caution that must be made immediately is that when we create a list or process, we must acknowledge that actual experience is never that easy, cut-and-dried, or predictable. The path to becoming a fully realized follower of Christ takes many twists and turns. My winding journey has taken me from dive bars, the Kennedy Center stage, and underneath a baobab tree in Zambia. So to even suggest that the path to true discipleship is a straight one is to expose yourself as one who has not stepped one foot on the journey. But something rings very true about the path laid out by these seven lessons. While people will encounter these seven powerful elements in very different ways, different stages, and way different orders, they still will have to encounter them all. Not only must they be encountered, but they must also be embraced as tools to be used in the service of building a deep relationship with Christ and his Kingdom.

So my encouragement is for you to meditate upon each of these seven powerful ideas. See if they ring true with scriptural witness. See if these concepts have an air of veracity as you look at the span of your life lived. Do you possess them? If so, celebrate and lean into them. If not, fight, scrap, claw, and work to make these seven lessons a part of your path. Engage this work with enthusiasm, knowing that passion and not passivity gains the day. Be gentle with yourself as you work toward making these concepts a part of your walk, and be gracious to yourself as these seven ideas, with fits and starts, ebbs and flows, and ups and downs, make their way into your daily practice. Never forget that love is the end game for all. Love is the fuel that fires the practice. Love is the agent that binds law to life. Love is the target for which you aim. Love is ultimately the proof of the miles traveled on the journey.

Has my developing faith and spiritual growth in Christ made me a more loving person? Can I receive and give love infinitely as the Infinite gives and receives? The answer to these questions determines the effectiveness of these first seven lessons of faith.

The race is on!!

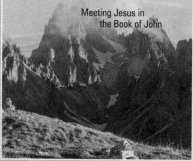
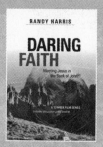